What people are saying about …

HOW TO RUIN YOUR CHILD IN 7 EASY STEPS

"Communication is extremely challenging and so very important. Patrick Quinn and Ken Roach use a backdoor method of communication to help parents apply truth. Instead of telling you what to do in raising your child, they come through the backdoor by telling you how to ruin your child. It is truth in reverse. Reading and applying the truths in this book will require great transparency and self-examination. But with your vices recognized and under control, your child's virtues can be recognized and practiced. Every reader will be challenged and blessed by this book."

Dr. John Ed Mathison, retired pastor and founder of John Ed Mathison Leadership Ministries

"Some books are stocking fillers—fun, light, and easy on the eyes. Some books are shoe fillers—hefty with wisdom and worthy of being added to a distinguished line of classics in the field. Patrick Quinn and Ken Roach have given us a rare and special gift: a book that fills up stockings *and* shoes."

Leonard Sweet, bestselling author, chief contributor to Sermons.com, and professor at Drew University, George Fox University, and Tabor College

"Being a dad can be downright daunting. I wonder what I'm doing wrong as a parent on a daily basis. Patrick and Ken bring much-needed clarity and encouragement to struggling moms and dads by reminding us that godly parenting is not easy … but it is simple: become the kind of person you want to reproduce."

Mark Stuart, cofounder of Audio Adrenaline
and the Hands and Feet Project

"If you google *parenting*, your computer blows up with links. Everybody has answers. What I love about this book is the timeless way it goes back to the scriptures and uses the seven deadly sins as a guide to help steer parents through the sea of parenting in our culture today. I especially like the chapter on pride—a major killer for dads today in effectively connecting to and leading their kids. I highly recommend this book to every parent."

Mitch Temple, family therapist, author,
Christian film consultant, and cofounder
of The Fatherhood CoMission

"Patrick Quinn has a rare ability to communicate inspirational insights from otherwise ordinary moments of parenthood. *How to Ruin Your Child in 7 Easy Steps* has the right amount of humor and humility, victories and failures, and above all, honesty, to be a great read for parents. This book not only makes me want to be a better father, but it gives me some tools to do so."

Roger W. Thompson, author of
My Best Friend's Funeral

"What a great, fresh, new perspective on parenting. With humility and humor from a man who is in the middle of raising his children, Patrick Quinn gives some wise direction to help us raise mature, responsible, spiritually alive kids. I wish this book had been available when I was in the trenches raising my children."

Dr. Tim Thompson, senior pastor of
Frazer United Methodist Church

"This faith-based parenting book tops my list! God's Word, interwoven throughout, lays a foundation for valuable tips and practical advice. Seven words describe this must-read for parents seeking to raise disciples of Jesus Christ: insightful, motivating, realistic, engaging, humorous, inspiring, and powerful!"

Glenda Argo, director of children's ministries
at First United Methodist Church

"Patrick Quinn and Ken Roach have written an excellent book that speaks directly to those who long to be more effective parents. While confessing that they do not have all of the answers, they have shared out of their own experiences the lessons that they have learned. Acknowledging the seven deadly sins that impact all of us, they offer practical suggestions of how to recognize these cardinal sins and triumph over them. Having closely observed Patrick and Rachael Quinn's parenting skills during these past twelve years, I can affirm that they 'practice what they preach.' You will become a more effective parent by reading, absorbing, and living out the lessons found within this book—I highly recommend it!"

Dr. Karl K. Stegall, retired minister of First
United Methodist Church and president of Stegall
Seminary Scholarship Endowment Foundation

"How to Ruin Your Child in 7 Easy Steps is a fun book to help parents develop character virtues in their children. It is based on the seven deadly sins of Proverbs 6:16–19 and their opposing virtues. Each chapter focuses on one of the deadly sins and grabs you immediately with a list of ways to ruin a child with that vice. The authors humorously and touchingly share from their life experience and give practical help on how to inculcate virtue into a child's life. This is a book I will enthusiastically give to the parents of my eight grandchildren!"

Jim Tomberlin, pastor, author, church consultant,
grandparent, and founder of MultiSite Solutions

HOW TO RUIN YOUR CHILD IN 7 EASY STEPS

TAME YOUR VICES, NURTURE THEIR VIRTUES

PATRICK M. QUINN
AND KEN ROACH

David C Cook®

transforming lives together

HOW TO RUIN YOUR CHILD IN 7 EASY STEPS
Published by David C Cook
4050 Lee Vance View
Colorado Springs, CO 80918 U.S.A.

David C Cook Distribution Canada
55 Woodslee Avenue, Paris, Ontario, Canada N3L 3E5

David C Cook U.K., Kingsway Communications
Eastbourne, East Sussex BN23 6NT, England

The graphic circle C logo is a registered trademark of David C Cook.

The website addresses recommended throughout this book are offered as a
resource to you. These websites are not intended in any way to be or imply an
endorsement on the part of David C Cook, nor do we vouch for their content.

LCCN 2014957980
ISBN 978-1-4347-0910-3
eISBN 978-1-4347-0932-5

The Team: Alex Field, LB Norton, Amy Konyndyk,
Nick Lee, Tiffany Thomas, Karen Athen
Cover Design: Amy Konyndyk
Cover Photo: iStockphoto

Printed in the United States of America
First Edition 2015

1 2 3 4 5 6 7 8 9 10

032815

CONTENTS

ACKNOWLEDGMENTS

One of the key messages of this book is that *how you parent* is really a function of *who you are*—everything about your own identity comes into play in how you influence your children's lives. So, in one sense, in order to give proper credit for a book on parenting, Ken and I need to acknowledge everyone who has ever played a role in shaping us into who we are today: our grandparents and parents, pastors and Sunday school teachers and youth leaders, mentors and professors. In another sense, there's nothing quite so audacious as writing a book on parenting, and if there's anything to find fault with in our book, no one is to blame but us!

With that said, we would like to offer special thanks to the team at Frazer United Methodist Church, whom we have the privilege of serving alongside every day and who afforded us the time to put these thoughts together in writing. A project like this certainly would not have been possible for me without the day-to-day work of my assistant, Rebecca Bright. The team at David C Cook publishing—including our editor, LB Norton, and copyeditor, Leigh Westin—have been wonderful to work with. Roger Thompson, whom I serendipitously met through a mission to serve orphans in Haiti, was responsible for helping us make our initial connection with the team at David C Cook. Most of all, we would like to thank our children. Kaylee, Cate, Patrick Wilson, Aubree, Ethan, Abbie, and Andrew—ultimately, we learn so much more from you than you ever learn from us. You are God's gifts to us, and we thank Him for the privilege of being earthly representatives of the Heavenly Father to you all.

Never forget that when we are dealing with any pleasure in its healthy and normal and satisfying form, we are, in a sense, on the Enemy's ground.... He made the pleasures: all our research so far has not enabled us to produce one. All we can do is to encourage the humans to take the pleasures which our Enemy has produced, at times, or in ways, or in degrees, which He has forbidden.

Advice from one demon to another, C. S. Lewis, *The Screwtape Letters*

He has granted to us his precious and very great promises, so that through them you may become partakers of the divine nature, having escaped from the corruption that is in the world because of sinful desire. For this very reason, make every effort to supplement your faith with virtue.

2 Peter 1:4–5

Chapter 1

I'VE GOT THIS

"I've got this," I told my wife one hot summer day in Fairhope, Alabama, when I pulled into the parking lot underneath the condo we'd rented. My wife, Rachael, and our children—teenager Kaylee, elementary-school-age Patrick Wilson, preschooler Cate, and baby Timothy,[1] our foster son at the time—were all eager to get started on our much-anticipated family vacation. It's not a long trip from central Alabama south to the Gulf of Mexico, but after a busy season of ministry, school, and extracurricular activities—the constant juggling act of family life—I was relieved to arrive for a few days of peace and relaxation. So, when I spotted a vacant parking space, I quickly sped toward it.

It didn't matter that the car on the left side was parked right on the line. It didn't matter that just to the right side was one of those giant concrete support columns. It didn't matter that I was driving my wife's minivan, which is a larger vehicle than what I usually drive.

"I've got this," I declared. After all, I had my aviator shades on. I may not have achieved my childhood dream of becoming a navy pilot, but I could land this van onto the carrier strip with all the swagger of a top gun pilot.

"I'm not sure you can make it in there, dear," Rachael said.

"Oh, I can make it. No problem."

"Are you sure? I just don't think this van is going to go in there."

"Maybe not if you were driving, but I've got this." (Yes, I actually said that to my wife, and we're still married. She is a remarkably forgiving woman.)

I trued it up between the lines and proceeded to put down the landing gear. But as we slowly eased into the gap, I heard a horrible sound—the unmistakable crunch of metal on concrete.

To her credit, Rachael said nothing. She is patient as well as forgiving. Or perhaps she's just really cunning. At that moment, I would have loved for her to say something smart, or even yell at me. Then I could have yelled back and made her the target of my frustration. Instead, her silence left me to stew in my own self-disgust.

The children, on the other hand, were not so quiet. Have you ever noticed kids can be completely oblivious to what you need them to see—the shoes lying right under their noses that they can't seem to find anywhere—and yet they instantly pick up on anything you wish they wouldn't notice?

"Hey, Dad, I think you hit something!"

"Hey, Dad, you're making the van go crunch!"

Thank you. Thank you very much for that news report. You all have a bright future in journalism.

The worst part was, there was nothing I could do but throw the car into reverse and back it up for another painfully long round of grinding metal before I could find another place to park. I jumped out to observe the damage—a four-foot long, scraped-up dent to the family ride.

For the next several months, like a scar from a wound, that scrape reminded me of the results of my ride with pride. Gradually, however, I came to realize this was not just a reminder that my parking skills weren't as great as I would've liked to think they were. Far more important, the scrape was a reminder that my parenting skills were not as great as I would've liked to think they were. How many times had my words, actions, or attitudes caused painful wounds to my wife or children? How has my pride led to scars on my family? And the whole time I was telling God, "I've got this."

The author of the book of Proverbs said it this way: "Trust in the LORD with all your heart, and do not rely on your own insight."[2] Or even more bluntly: "Do you see persons wise in their own eyes? There is more hope for fools than for them."[3]

Bottom line: when we tell God, "I've got this, I don't need Your help," whether in the area of parenting or any other area of life, we're in trouble.

Maybe as you read my story, you thought of some scars you've left on your family. Maybe you spoke to your daughter in anger just this morning and are now wondering what the long-term effects of your words will be on her self-esteem. Maybe you brushed your son off last night because you were too busy to spend time with him and are now wondering how many times you can do that before he stops asking. Or perhaps you've already been through a major trauma in your family—divorce, dealing with a rebellious teen or child who gets into trouble with drugs or crime.

Lest you give up in despair and put this book down without reading it, please allow me to say, this book's title is tongue in cheek. You can't actually ruin your child. Not that parents don't sometimes do terrible things. We do. But God's grace is greater. He can turn even our worst messes into something beautiful.

Like an experienced guide in a dangerous jungle, God has given us tools that can help us identify and avoid some of the worst parenting pitfalls. The wisdom of God unfolded in the Bible and the experiences of others who have gone before us mark out a trail for us. Both provide us with a map that can guide us around those lurking dangers.

One such map is the church tradition of listing the seven deadly sins. In one form or another, this list has been around since the early centuries of Christianity. They are generally known today as pride, lust, envy, greed, gluttony, sloth, and wrath. They are called deadly or mortal sins, not because a person will drop dead the moment any are committed, but because each sin has the effect of turning one's heart away from God's love and grace, thus damaging the spiritual life within, leading down a path toward destruction. In the battle of parenthood, these sins are mortal enemies.

The big seven are also known as capital sins—literally, *head* sins—because so many little sins grow out of them. They are like cancers that grow within us and cause all kinds of side effects and surface symptoms. On the negative side, that means these seven tend to snowball—once they start, they get bigger and bigger. On the positive side, it means that if we can learn to avoid them, we can cut off the head of the snake that could strangle our spiritual growth before it coils around our lives and the lives of our children.

THE RELATIONSHIP EQUATION

Do you remember taking algebra in school (or reviewing it while you tried to help your kids with their homework)? The one essential principle is, whatever operation you perform on one side of the equation, you have perform the same operation on the other side. If you add to the left side, you must add to the right side; if you subtract from the right side, you must subtract from the left side, and so on.

The same principle holds true in the equation of human relationships: whatever affects one person also affects the other. But in human relationships, you don't have the power to directly change the other side of the equation. People resist being changed, but that doesn't mean you can't change yourself. And when you change yourself, you change the equation.

Jesus said, "Do not judge, and you will not be judged; do not condemn, and you will not be condemned. Forgive, and you will be forgiven; give, and it will be given to you. A good measure, pressed down, shaken together, running over, will be put into your lap; for the measure you give will be the measure you get back."[4]

That's why, as I offer practical principles on how you can teach your children to avoid the seven deadly sins, I will continually return to the importance of learning how to overcome them yourself.

Leading by example is not just a good suggestion; it's a fact of nature. Regardless of our words, our children tend to become like us. Some of the most terrifying words of Jesus for any parent are these: "Can a blind person guide a blind person? Will not both fall into a pit? A disciple is not above the teacher, but everyone who is fully qualified will be like the teacher."[5]

To paraphrase, your children are likely to make the same mistakes you do. If you don't conquer lust, chances are your son won't either. If you fall victim to envy, your daughter probably will too. If you don't conquer a sin, don't expect them to overcome it either. Maybe that doesn't scare you, but it sure scares me!

But here's the positive side of the same truth: When you invest time in changing yourself—even a little bit—it gives you enormous leverage to influence change in your children.

This should give us hope. Our power to change ourselves, and through that change to wield influence in our children's lives, is incredibly strong. "Everyone who is fully qualified will be like the teacher." So change the teacher, and you'll change the student. Change the parent, and you'll change the child.

THE FLIP SIDE

Each of the seven sins has a corresponding cardinal virtue, a habit of the heart we can nourish in our families into a healthy faith life. In the following chapters, we'll discuss how easy it is to practice vices and unintentionally hand them over to our children. Even better, we will discover how, with a little intentional planning, an ample helping of old-fashioned hard work, and God's grace, we can replace those vices with virtues. We can choose to ruin our children in seven easy steps or build them a seven-fold foundation of lasting significance.

And please understand: I'm not writing this book because I have all the answers. I struggle with these seven sins as much as the next person (the scar on the side of my van reminds me of that). Simply by opening this book, you've shown an openness to hear from God about parenting, and I believe He will honor you by speaking throughout these pages. When God speaks, you can choose to trust in the Lord with all your heart, or you can say, "I've got this."

With that in mind, let's start our journey together with a prayer.

Heavenly Father, thank You for the incredible privilege and high calling of parenthood. I admit I don't know what I'm doing; my human understanding is not enough for the enormous task of raising the intricately designed children You have given to me in this dangerous and difficult world.

I ask You to give me Your wisdom. Keep me from pride and the other sins that destroy Your plan for my life and bring hurt and pain to my family. Bring Your mercy and healing to the scars I have already caused. Give me faith to see the beautiful future You have in store for us.

I commit my family to You; show me Your path. I will trust in You because I know You love me, and You love my children even more than I do. In Jesus's name. Amen.

Chapter 2

I'M NOT THE PROBLEM

The Deadly Sin of Pride

10 WAYS TO RUIN YOUR CHILD THROUGH PRIDE

1. Build your life around yourself. It's all about you.
2. Never *show* your kids how to live, just *tell* them.
3. When you meet resistance, work on the rules first, not the relationship.
4. Never doubt yourself. You've got this. You don't need anyone else.
5. Remind your children that you're better than they are—at everything. It builds character.
6. Never admit you were wrong. You will lose respect if you're not constantly perfect.
7. Church is for weak people. You're strong enough to do this without God.
8. Don't answer to anyone. Push away any friend who starts to question you.
9. Find ways to get others to serve you. You deserve it.
10. Other people have pride problems, not you.

RIDING THE BRAKES

Since that day in the parking garage, my daughter Kaylee turned sixteen, and thus began the process of teaching her to drive. There's nothing more thrilling nor more terrifying than hurtling through space with a teen at the wheel—like being on my own personal roller coaster.

It's amazing how many things we take for granted about driving until we try to teach someone else. For instance, the subtleties of that little pedal in the middle of the floorboard called the brake. Maybe we should rename it the whiplash button.

A law of physics, of which I grew newly aware, is you have to be moving to steer. At first Kaylee wanted to separate the two—get her wheels all lined up before she hit the gas. I kept reminding her, "You have to start moving first, then cut your wheel at the same time." It's a struggle to turn while sitting still; it's easy when you're moving. It's just an exercise in faith.

Now here's the life lesson for parents. Your relationship with your children is the gas; teaching and discipline are the wheel. It's tempting to want to correct your children first and think about investing time in relationship with them later, after you get things all lined up. But that doesn't really work. It's extremely difficult to turn a vehicle that's not moving.

I see parents all the time who are working very hard to correct their children, but they don't realize it doesn't have to be so hard. If they would invest more time in building a relationship—hit the gas a little harder—they would discover it's much easier to steer.

That analogy poses the question: What gets in the way of building a relationship? Sometimes we blame our lack of time, because we're just too busy. In the analogy, that's like running out of gas. Other times we blame our children's stubbornness. They don't want a relationship with us and push us away. That's like having a flat tire. We're not going anywhere until we pull off to the side of our paths and change an attitude or two.

Both our lack of time and their stubbornness can be factors in why the relationship isn't gaining much acceleration. However, I'd like to suggest another reason, one I think is actually much more common than we recognize. Many parents are riding down the road with one foot on the gas and the other foot on the brake. And the name of that brake pedal is pride.

Three times in God's Word, pride is linked to resistance.[1] Peter and James both tell us, "God opposes the proud, but gives grace to the humble." The writer of Proverbs says, "Toward the scorners he is scornful, but to the humble he gives favor." I don't know about you, but I'm thinking that if God says something three times, it must be really important to Him. Here's my paraphrase: in a relationship with God, humility hits the gas and pride hits the brakes.

God warns us repeatedly about pride because it destroys our relationship with Him. God does not want your life to implode into self-centeredness like a black hole that collapses into nothingness under its own gravity. But it's pretty hard to worship your Creator when you are High Priest of My Way in the Temple of Me.

And there's another good reason why God repeats the pride warning—He isn't the only one who resists the proud. Think for a moment about that arrogant boss you once worked for or that stuck-up kid at school or the preacher who thought he was better than everyone else. Were you drawn to those people, or did you instinctively push away from them?

On the other hand, I'm willing to bet that if you think about the people in your life you have really been drawn to—the coach you played your hardest for, the friend you felt the most relaxed with, the Christian leader you were inspired to be like—they shared a common trait of deep-down, genuine humility.

POWER AND INFLUENCE

As moms and dads, we have a degree of power over our children, and it's important we use that power wisely. But that power grows more and more limited as our children grow older. Our *influence* over our children, however, is virtually unlimited and has the potential to inspire change in their hearts and minds.

Influence does not come from formal authority or power. You might force others to change their *behavior*, but you will never reach their hearts and minds. So how do we gain influence? One of my favorite writers, Henri Nouwen, says it this way: "What makes the temptation of power so seemingly irresistible? Maybe it is that power offers an easy substitute for the hard task of love. It seems easier to be God than to love God, easier to control people than to love people, easier to own life than to love life."[2]

In other words, influence flows out of relationship.

One place I've seen this principle at work in my own life is on the ball field. I'm an old baseball player, good enough for some college ball but not quite good enough to make it to the minor leagues. I love the game, so naturally I love sharing it with my children, especially my son, Patrick Wilson. As PW works his way up through Little League, one of the lessons I want him to learn is how to handle losing. I want him to be a good sport but at the same time be motivated to learn from his mistakes and get better. There is a delicate balance between caring too much about a game, thus losing your temper, and not caring enough, thus lacking motivation to improve.

I can preach long and hard to PW about how to achieve this balance, but where the rubber meets the road is not when he is on the field; it's when he is in the stands watching me play in men's league for the church team. When my team loses or an umpire makes a bad call, all my sermons go out the window. I want to yell and throw my bat. I'm thinking, *Why does my name have to be on the back of my jersey, so everyone has to know I'm the preacher!* That's when I realize, though, not only is the whole town watching to see how the minister acts on the ball field, but my son is watching. If I want to have a positive influence on him, it starts with humbling myself. As hard as it may be to control my emotions at times, it's a whole lot easier than trying to control his! If I want to change PW, I have to start with changing me.

JUST LIKE ME

Prideful people judge, condemn, withhold love, and refuse to forgive—treatment they tend to receive in return. Prideful parents control, manipulate, bully, and lie to their children, and in return they tend to earn rebellion, defiance, detachment, and deception.

Okay, wait a minute. It's time for me to throw the emergency brake on this book and challenge you directly. As you read the previous paragraph, were you thinking about someone who really needs to hear those words? Maybe your own parents came to mind. Maybe a friend who has problems with his or her children. Maybe you were wishing your husband or wife would read this message.

All of those people may very well have a real problem with pride, but can you see how prideful it is to think about them but not yourself? The most consistent symptom of pride is self-deception. After all, "the heart is deceitful above all things, and desperately sick; who can understand it?"[3] Pride is easy to see in others but almost impossible to see in yourself.

Maybe that's why Jesus posed this question: "Why do you see the speck in your neighbor's eye, but do not notice the log in your own eye? Or how can you say to your neighbor, 'Friend, let me take out the speck in your eye,' when you yourself do not see the log in your own eye? You hypocrite, first take the log out of your own eye, and then you will see clearly to take the speck out of your neighbor's eye."[4]

Jesus isn't just calling us out for being hypocrites. He's trying to show us the way to have real influence in the lives of others, including those closest to us. He understands how our relationships really work, because He created us.

Part of what hides our pride is that we can come up with dozens of self-justifying stories to explain away our own behavior and never recognize the root problem as pride.

- "That's just the way I am."
- "That's the way I was raised."
- "I'm doing the best I can."
- "I meant well."
- "My intentions were good."
- "I was just having a bad day."
- "People misunderstand me."

But God sees through our stories. Scripture warns us, "If we say we have no sin, we deceive ourselves, and the truth is not in us."[5]

Here's a little quiz to help identify areas where you might struggle with pride:

When someone criticizes me, do I immediately look for the grain of truth in the critique, or do I focus on defending myself?

When someone praises me, do I immediately think of other people who helped me succeed?

When I realize I am wrong, do I quickly and sincerely apologize?

When someone contradicts my opinion, am I more concerned with being right or with possibly learning something new?

Do I become quickly irritated with others who interrupt me, slow me down, or pull me off schedule?

Am I willing to take on lowly jobs or those viewed as less important than others?

Am I willing to spend time with people who might be viewed by some as lowly or unimportant?

Do I become irritated when I do something for others and don't receive a thank-you?

Is it important to me for others to always think of me as humble?

Am I overly sensitive to little things other people do or say that indicate arrogance or pride?

Or here's an even simpler rule of thumb: if you found yourself getting defensive when I suggested you may have a problem with pride, you have a problem with pride. I can say that with confidence because *all* of us have a problem with pride. The question is not whether pride is an issue. The question is, how will we handle it?

LET'S GO FOR A RUN

I'll never forget the day Kaylee and I went running in our Gulf Shores, Alabama, neighborhood when she was twelve. Overall, it was a day like many others. We had been enjoying sports together since she was seven years old and running together for much of that time. It was a great opportunity to spend time together, build our relationship, and get in a little exercise to boot. What was different that day was I could tell she was ready to leave me behind.

In my mind's eye, I can still see the spot where we were running, about two miles from home. In the past I had always set the pace, but this time I was starting to get winded, while Kaylee showed no signs of slowing down. Before I really even knew what I was doing, I said to her, "Do you want to run on ahead?" She looked at me with a question in her eyes for half a second, then smiled. "Sure, Dad!" And she was off, heading back to the house, leaving me behind. Panic gripped me briefly. *What have I done?* I wondered.

Yet at the same time I realized, this was always where we had been heading. In the words of John the Baptist to Jesus, "He must increase, I must decrease." That's true for us as parents too. The day comes when our children become adults and leave us behind. We may dread it and even feel sad when that day comes, but in our hearts that's what we truly want for them. They must increase, we must decrease. But when they leave us behind, what will they take with them? An old Jewish blessing says, "May the dust of your rabbi be upon you." It means may you be following so closely in your teacher's footsteps that who he or she is rubs off on you, and you become like that person.

Kaylee was leaving me in the dust, but in other ways she was carrying my dust with her. After all the miles she had run behind me, in my footsteps, my influence had rubbed off on her, and she will always carry that with her, no matter how far ahead of me she eventually goes. And my prayer is that she will go far indeed.

Get Practical: Four Ways to Humble Yourself

Here are four practical ways you can put pride away and start leveraging the power of influence.

1. Confess when you are wrong and ask for forgiveness.

Nothing demolishes pride faster than admitting you were wrong, but that's not easy for parents. We operate on the principle, "You're never wrong if you don't admit you're wrong!" However, our children see right through that. Apologizing to them isn't going to surprise them with the news that you make mistakes; they already know that. What will surprise them is your willingness to own up to it. Many times I've had to kneel down beside the bed of one of my children at night and ask for forgiveness because I overcorrected based on my pride. It's humbling, but I know I have to do it to restore that relationship, without which I can never have true influence in their lives.

2. Center yourself in worship.

Worship is a regular opportunity to remind yourself that there's something bigger than you are. It's a map check, like a big red arrow that says, "You are here—and here is not the center of the universe." Through singing praises, sharing prayers, speaking the liturgy, and hearing God's Word proclaimed, worship has the power to humble us, not by putting ourselves down but by refreshing our picture of how big God is. Along the way, as your children see you in worship, you will be modeling for them how to live a life of humility instead of pride.

3. Connect to an accountability group.

Children are accountable to their parents, but all too often in our culture we believe the lie that adults don't have to be accountable to anyone. We call it freedom, but freedom from accountability is like the freedom of driving on a dangerous mountain road and removing the guardrails. Accountability grows out of a relationship of trust with a small group of like-minded people. Accountability simply means you give certain people permission to ask you the tough questions about how you are doing in your walk with God and what you are doing with your life. Pride hates to be questioned. Humility considers it an honor, a badge of love, for someone to care enough to ask questions. The wisdom of Proverbs says, "Do not reprove a scoffer, or he will hate you; reprove a wise man, and he will love you."[6]

4. Commit yourself to service.

When you take time to meet the needs of others without thought of personal reward, you reconnect to the essence of love. Especially when you can find ways to serve in secret—working behind the scenes, giving anonymously, doing random acts of kindness for a stranger who will never even know who did it—you kill pride at the root. Service is like Roundup for your soul—it kills the weeds of pride and selfishness. Pride wants to be served, or at least to be seen serving; humility simply wants what is best for others. This is particularly important if you have a position of authority at work or in the community—the more you become a "big deal," the more you need to get away and serve others in simple, direct ways. After all, Jesus took time out to wash His disciples' feet.[7] I doubt you are a bigger deal than He is.

As we move forward through the remaining six deadly sins, we'll continue to revisit the importance of resisting pride. It will be a good thing to remind ourselves that, figuratively speaking, eventually we'll all be looking at our children's backs as they run on ahead of us. May each of us invest the time, energy, and attention on them we ought to, so when that moment comes, we can rejoice knowing they will carry with them our dust and loving influence born from humility.

Chapter 3

IF IT FEELS GOOD, IT MUST BE GOOD

The Deadly Sin of Lust

10 WAYS TO RUIN YOUR CHILD'S LIFE THROUGH LUST

1. If you want it, get it now. Sooner is always better.
2. Doing whatever feels good is true freedom.
3. Talk to your kids about how mean God is and how much He hates fun.
4. Talk about marriage as if it were a prison so your kids will know they need to sow their wild oats as much as possible now.
5. Give rules without reasons.
6. Teach your kids that sex is all about the body. It has nothing to do with the heart, mind, emotions, or spirit.
7. Watch whatever you want. What you look at has no effect on your heart.
8. Secrets are safe. As long as you don't get caught, no one will get hurt.
9. You can handle temptation. Get as close as possible to prove how strong you are.
10. If you get hooked on something, don't tell anyone. You can fix it on your own.

DON'T JUST SAY NO

Brandon is a divorced friend who has remarried. His teenage son, Colin,[1] was planning to visit him during the summer break, and Brandon was hoping to reconnect during their time together since he had noticed Colin drifting away emotionally for some time. When Colin arrived, however, things only got worse. The boy was distant, apathetic, and lethargic. He slept most of the day and had almost no interaction with his stepmother or younger siblings.

Then one day Brandon had a difficult conversation with Colin. It was awkward and painful. But after that day—Brandon says it happened within twenty-four hours—Colin was a different person. He was smiling and laughing. He made jokes with his stepmother. He played with his brother and sister. He even stayed awake more. It was as if he had come back to life.

What happened during that conversation?

We'll come back to Brandon and Colin's story later, but before we do, we need to get some things straight right from the start. When we talk about overcoming the deadly sin of lust, we're not talking about learning to say no to all of our desires. We're not talking about becoming so spiritual we have no more physical drives. In the Christian worldview, physical pleasure is a good thing. Overcoming lust is not about getting rid of pleasure. It's about getting greater pleasure—more life, more joy—by learning how to govern our bodies and emotions in a way that gets the right pleasure at the right time.

If there's one thing we parents say to our children more than "no," it's probably "not right now." Sometimes it seems parenthood is one long, extended battle to teach our children the simple principle of delayed gratification:

- "Put the snack down now so you can enjoy the delicious, healthy meal later."
- "Do the hard work in practice today so you can enjoy winning the game later."
- "Study hard now so you can do more meaningful work later."

Although it is hard for a parent to delay answering the demands of a child, we often see that children are happier and healthier when we keep them on a schedule rather than always gratifying their desires instantly. Life is all about these trades between a small pleasure today and a greater pleasure later on.

I learned this early on from my dad in, of all places, a bowling alley. He played in a league, and I would tag along. But I was not focused on the strikes and spares. My eyes were drawn to the blinking lights of the video arcade games along the wall. So my dad made me a proposal: Each visit he would give me a quarter. It was mine to spend on a game, if I so chose. However, if I held on to my quarter and didn't spend it, at the end of the evening he would give me another quarter. Some weeks I gave in and spent my quarter right away. But most of the time I held out for that delayed gratification. It didn't take me long to discover—once I had saved up a few quarters—I could bring one of my own to play the game and still save his quarter to get the reward. At ten years old, I was already living off the interest.

The delayed-gratification lesson my dad taught me has served me well. I'm no investment genius, but I've been able to do reasonably well in the investment world by following the Warren Buffet principles of buying stock companies you're knowledgeable of at value prices and holding them for the long haul, instead of pursuing penny stocks and day trading on speculation. (It probably helps that my accountant wife knows a lot about money management.) The point is, I'm still doing what my dad taught me: hold on to that quarter, not because a game is bad, but because I can get a greater return later if I wait.

THE CREATOR OF PLEASURE

If we understand this principle for our children, how much more God must understand it for us. As Jesus said, "If you then, who are evil, know how to give good gifts to your children, how much more will your Father who is in heaven give good things to those who ask him!"[2]

Unfortunately, along the way we've gotten into the trap of thinking God is against pleasure. Satan has become the author of fun and God the cosmic killjoy. We've been led to believe that lust means wanting something really badly, so being a good, spiritual person must mean making myself not want anything—or at least never giving into temptation.

However, the God of the Bible is not against physical pleasure. In Genesis we learn He created Adam with an earthly body, along with all of its desires, and called that body "very good."[3] God affirmed the essential goodness of our physicality by sending His son Jesus to be incarnate—made flesh—through Mary. He then affirmed it again when He raised Christ from the dead, not as a ghost or spirit, but with a glorified but nevertheless solid, real, physical body, capable of being touched and of eating real food.[4]

Food, drink, recreation, and yes, sex, are all pleasures for us because we were created that way by God. He wants us to enjoy them. When we buy into the false idea that God doesn't want us to have fun, we are left with two dead-end choices: either we reject God as the cosmic killjoy and completely disregard the "outdated rules of morality," or we grit our teeth and try our best to please this angry deity, limping along with the deep frustration of feeling guilty every time we enjoy ourselves. It's not hard to see that as a parenting philosophy, either of those choices is a clear pathway to ruining your child. Behind door number one is an unplanned pregnancy, STD, or drug addiction; behind door number two is a hefty therapy bill for your kid.

DESIRE AND FAITH

So if God does not teach that desire is bad, why all the rules and restrictions in the Bible, especially in the area of sexuality? If sex is natural, why can't we just sleep with whomever we want, whenever we want? Increasingly in our society, that is the question being asked, and all too often Christian parents are left with the religious version of "because I said so." We don't know why, but it's in the Bible, so that's the way it is. The problem is, when you don't know why you believe what you believe, it's a whole lot harder to teach those beliefs to someone else. Especially your hormone-infused teenager.

The answer is, God teaches that desire is good, but He does not want us to substitute a lesser good for a greater good. We read in the letter to the Hebrews that "without faith it is impossible to please him, for whoever would draw near to God must believe that he exists and that he rewards those who seek him."[5] Did you catch that? God expects us to desire rewards. But He wants us to go beyond the immediate rewards we can see to the greater rewards that can only be visualized by faith.

Here are a couple of metaphors to help us grasp this. In the world of food there are simple sugars and complex sugars. Simple sugars take very little work for the body to break down, and they give us an immediate hit of pleasure on the taste buds. Unfortunately, they also have a way of wrecking our health. Candy, sweets, highly processed foods, and fast food tend to be loaded with simple sugars. The more complex sugars found in fruits, vegetables, whole grains, and organic foods are better for us, but they take more work to prepare.

Or consider the world of music. A simple, catchy little melody can get stuck in your head for days. Music producers call this a hook. We hear it, we love it, we want some more of it. Over time, though, those simple tunes become boring, and we have to seek out the newest hook to replace them; they don't tend to become the timeless, enduring classics we could listen to again and again. Great music, on the other hand, is usually built by layering simple melodies into complex arrangements and harmonies. It takes more effort to understand and appreciate a piece by Bach (or for that matter, U2's album *War* or Marvin Gaye's song "What's Going On") than, say, Carly Rae Jepsen's song "Call Me Maybe."

It's not that simple pleasures are bad in and of themselves. It's just that they tend to crowd out higher pleasures, and knowing God is the highest pleasure of all. Pastor and theologian John Piper argues in his book *Desiring God* for what he calls "Christian hedonism"—the idea that worship flows out of love, and love for God comes from recognizing by faith that He is the most lovely, beautiful, desirable source of joy in all the universe.[6] When we truly understand who God is, we will desire Him more than anything else. We won't be drawn to lesser gods when we see the light of His glory.

BECOMING LESS THAN HUMAN

Returning to the realm of sexuality, this principle of the greater pleasure is why God warns us over and over about the danger of immorality. It's not that God is antisex. He created sex. It's His idea. Sexuality is part of our humanity, and our Creator wants us to be unabashedly human. But precisely because He created it, He understands the enormous power it has and how destructive that power can be if we twist and distort sexuality away from His original design.

In fact, throughout the Bible illicit sexuality is always connected with idolatry. Idolatry is the practice of worshipping something less than God as if it were God. And the catch is, we always become like what we worship. When we worship the true God, we become the most fully human. But when we worship idols, we become less human—like animals, only worse, because at least animals are supposed to be animals. We become a dingy, distorted, empty shell of what God created us to be.

The dehumanizing influence of idolatry and immorality are tied together by the apostle Paul in his letter to the Romans:

> For although they knew God, they did not honor him as God or give thanks to him, but they became futile in their thinking, and their foolish hearts were darkened. Claiming to be wise, they became fools, and exchanged the glory of the immortal God for images resembling mortal man and birds and animals and creeping things.
>
> Therefore God gave them up in the lusts of their hearts to impurity, to the dishonoring of their bodies among themselves, because they exchanged the truth about God for a lie and worshiped and served the creature rather than the Creator, who is blessed forever! Amen.[7]

Notice that the punishment for sin is not some arbitrary plague from heaven; rather, it is that God "gave them up" to their own lusts. Paul is speaking here of the enslaving nature of addiction. This is the beautiful and terrible mystery of free will: God loves us too much to force us to love Him; we are given the choice. Once we make the initial choice, though, we will tend to fall under the power of habit. It gets easier to make the same choice in our next decision and correspondingly harder to change.

When we keep God as our first and highest pleasure, we can enjoy all the other pleasures in their due and proper measure. However, when we reject God and choose to worship other pleasures, pretty soon those pleasures end up owning us. We become slaves to our own bodies.

Which is why sexual ethics are more than just cultural constructs. Ever since the sexual revolution of the 1960s, Christian teachings on immorality have been under attack, reaching a fever pitch in the more recent debates over homosexual marriage. Whatever we may believe about the legal issues of gay rights, we can't buy into the idea that sex is just whatever we want to make of it. Sexuality is part of our bodies, and our bodies were created by God, not ourselves. As Paul wrote on another occasion,

> For this is the will of God, your sanctification: that you abstain from sexual immorality; that each one of you know how to control his own body in holiness and honor, not in the passion of lust like the Gentiles who do not know God; that no one transgress and wrong his brother in this matter, because the Lord is an avenger in all these things, as we told you beforehand and solemnly warned you. For God has not called us for impurity, but in holiness. Therefore whoever disregards this, disregards not man but God, who gives his Holy Spirit to you.[8]

This is not some prudish old lady wagging her finger at us and trying to make us feel frightened of our own sexuality. This is the Creator God, who loves us and desires what is best for us, pointing us away from self-destructive paths to the greater pleasures of either monogamous marriage or celibate singleness.

HOOKED BY THE EYES

No parents say to their kids, "One day you'll fall in love and get married, but if you see someone else at work who's hot, you can always sneak around and commit adultery. Don't let commitment get in the way of what feels good." No one says that, just as no one says, "Have you thought about becoming addicted to meth when you grow up, little Johnny? It sure feels good when you're high!" or "Alcoholism—now there's a path to true happiness." We don't say that. Or do we?

Remember, your greatest point of leverage in changing your child's life is to change yourself. So let me just come right out and challenge you on the biggest issue I see in our day when it comes to lust. Mom or Dad, are you teaching your sons and daughters to be sexually pure with their bodies but are secretly hooked on pornography?

In my role as pastor, I frequently see couples who are on their way toward divorce. In so many cases, porn is a huge part of the problem. Sometimes a husband brings a porn addiction from his teenage or college years into the marriage, and it has distorted his understanding of what married sex should look like. Other times, some other issue hinders the couple from physical intimacy, and the husband turns to porn for relief, only to find that this short-term solution only makes the long-term problems worse.

According to X3church, an online ministry dedicated to freeing people from pornography addiction, about forty million Americans are sexually involved with the Internet. Two-thirds of men in their twenties and thirties report they regularly visit porn sites. And this may surprise you, but statistically, an increasing number of porn addicts are also women, with more than a third of churchgoing women reporting they have intentionally visited porn websites.[9]

Whatever the cause, it is tragic to see this drama play out again and again. This seemingly innocent, seemingly victimless crime of looking at inappropriate pictures (or reading inappropriate stories) offers a quick hit of sexual pleasure, the simple sugar of sex, only to undermine and destroy the true pleasures of emotional and spiritual intimacy and ultimately destroy entire families. And the ones who are hurt most are the children.

THE SECRET IS OUT

Even in cases where the secret never comes out, we still reap what we sow when it comes to immorality. Consider the case of King David. You probably know the story of how the great shepherd king, the "man after God's own heart," drifted away from his walk of faith and ended up committing adultery with Bathsheba.[10] God confronts David's sin through the prophet Nathan, and David repents in one of the most moving confessions in all of the Bible (read Psalm 51).

Nevertheless, the scars of his sin remain. Years later, his son Amnon falls in lust with his half sister Tamar and eventually rapes her, yet David does nothing to bring him to justice. Furious, Tamar's older brother Absalom swears to take revenge on David. Absalom murders Amnon and ultimately stages a full-scale rebellion against his own father, chasing David out of Jerusalem with an army. Then, in one of the sickest acts recorded in Scripture, he publicly rapes his father's concubines.

The question is, why did David do nothing when Amnon violated his sister, David's daughter? The Bible doesn't say, but if we read between the lines, it doesn't seem too crazy to suggest it was David's guilt over his own sin with Bathsheba that made him feel unworthy to discipline his son. Likewise, this may have been the reason he did not take more direct action to stop Absalom before he plunged the whole kingdom into war.

Parents who harbor secret sins often discipline their children inconsistently. They may be unreasonably lenient, allowing things they know they should not because they feel hypocritical imposing a standard they themselves are not living up to. For example, a dad might tell his wife there is nothing wrong with their son looking at the *Sports Illustrated* swimsuit edition because "it's just part of being a boy," when what he really means is he doesn't want to be held accountable for the stuff he looks at either.

Other times, parents may be excessively strict, projecting their own guilt onto their children and harshly punishing them. Or they may vacillate between lenient and strict so the son or daughter doesn't know what to expect. An example would be the double-standard dad who encourages his son to check out girls but becomes furious when his daughter wears immodest clothing.

The bottom line when it comes to discipline is this: we must first be honest about our own secret sins before we can objectively help our children deal with theirs. As Paul said it, "Dear brothers and sisters, if another believer is overcome by some sin, you who are godly should gently and humbly help that person back onto the right path. And be careful not to fall into the same temptation yourself."[11] Remember, the basis of our discipline is not ourselves, but God's Word. Our past failures don't disqualify us from disciplining our children today.

ADDICTIONS BIG AND SMALL

In today's culture, we usually call a problem with lust an addiction. The interesting thing is that brain scientists are discovering similar patterns at work in all kinds of behaviors.[12] There are the well-known addictions of alcohol and habit-forming drugs, but people also become addicted to playing video games, to gambling, to eating, and even to working out. The factors they have in common are a quick hit of easy pleasure that hooks us right off the bat, but then we have to continually do more in order to get that same initial high. The addictive behavior starts to take over our lives, displacing other forms of healthy pleasure and disrupting relationships. This, in turn, creates a vicious cycle as we turn to the addiction for relief from the pain caused by the addiction.

Some types of addiction can be managed without wrecking one's entire life, but the problem is, what we allow in moderation, our children tend to excuse in excess. They see what we value and conclude that if a little is good, more must be better. Nothing is more heartbreaking than to watch a child drowning in destructive habits because he or she dove headfirst into the sin that a parent merely dabbled a foot in.

- "Hey, Mom, I saw that you managed your stress with alcohol, so I've decided to manage my stress with cocaine."
- "Hey, Dad, I saw that you put off doing tasks around the house to just watch TV, so I've decided to put off getting a job so I can play video games all day."
- "Hey, Mom, I saw that you escaped into the world of sexual romance novels, so I've decided to escape by having an affair with an older, married man."
- "Hey, Dad, I saw that you didn't turn your eyes away from the Victoria's Secret models and scantily clad NFL cheerleaders, so I've decided not to turn my eyes away from hard-core porn."

And so it goes.

THE REST OF THE STORY

So what happened in that conversation between my friend Brandon and his son, Colin? Brandon discovered Colin had been secretly looking at pornography on his computer and confronted him. Colin admitted that, back at his mother's house, he had succumbed to the temptation for months. It had become a habit that dominated his life.

Overcoming that habit would be a journey for Colin. Together he and Brandon put steps into place, like monitoring Colin's web usage and moving his computer into the living room. However, the overnight transformation in his demeanor was a result of the tremendous burden of secrecy being lifted from Colin's soul.

Brandon was able to approach Colin with grace and humility because he had struggled with pornography himself at one point but turned to God for deliverance. He was able to share with his son how he had taken practical steps to reduce temptation and how the accountability of Christian brothers helped him to stay on track. Most of all, he was able to share hope with his son. He could say with authenticity, "This will be a struggle, but you can fight this battle and win. I know, because I've experienced God's victory myself."

Get Practical: Three Steps to Breaking the Chain

So how do we confront the sin of lust so it does not ruin our lives and our children's lives? Let me suggest three steps to get you started on the journey to freedom.

1. Believe in hope.

In whatever area lust may have a grip on your life and to whatever degree it has enslaved you, there is always hope. The great lie we are tempted to believe is, we can't get free so we might as well give up trying—especially when we've tried before to break a habit but have fallen back into it. God created you to be fully human, filled with His freedom, love, and life. It's a lie that says, "This is just the way I am; I can't do anything about it." Lust is not who you are.

The truth is, our own willpower is not enough to break the most binding chains of lust, but the power of Christ is. Freedom can be a long journey, but it is possible because Christ died to free us from our sins—not just one day when we go to heaven, but right here, right now. As we read in Scripture, "If God is for us, who can ever be against us? Since he did not spare even his own Son but gave him up for us all, won't he also give us everything else?"[13]

It's vital that we communicate this hope to our children. Many times children come to believe that if they ever fall, there's no way they can get up. This is true not only for the wild-child types but especially for the rule followers. They live in fear of messing up and often feel guilty for just being tempted, even if they don't give in. We need to share grace with them. Scripture says, "The righteous falls seven times and rises again."[14] The message to our sons and daughters needs to be, "I want you to avoid the hurt and pain that comes from sin, but I also want you to know there is always forgiveness, and where there is forgiveness, there is always hope."

2. Don't be a hero.

Another lie we are led to believe is that if we are spiritual enough, we should be able to put ourselves into a tempting situation and not have a problem. After all, Jesus said sin comes from the heart, not from the environment, right? Not at all. Part of having a "pure heart" is the willingness to remove ourselves from situations that we know are too much for us to handle. Paul's advice to his young protégé Timothy was simple and direct: "Flee also youthful lusts."[15]

If watching certain TV shows, getting online in certain situations, or driving past certain places gets you in trouble, change the channel, get off the computer, drive a different route. There's nothing shameful about running from temptation. Remember, God resists the proud but gives grace to the humble, and admitting when we are tempted is part of humility.

Children need us to walk them through what this looks like. Before you send them to spend the night at a friend's house, for example, try role-playing with them. Show your child exactly what to say and do if that friend wants to watch something on TV or online that is inappropriate. It's not enough to say, "Just say no to drugs." We need to give our children precise steps of action on how to say no and what their options are after they say no, whether it's to drugs, alcohol, porn, or anything else their conscience tells them is wrong.

3. Get help.

The great power of lust lies in its secrecy. Dark things grow in dark places. Coming out into the light is your most powerful step in the right direction. I'm not saying you have to wear a T-shirt around town that says I Have a Lust Problem. However, you need to come clean to those closest to you who are affected by your sin (and they are always affected), and you need to find a group of peers or a wise mentor you can trust to hold you accountable.

I've never known anyone who decided to keep an addictive behavior secret who ultimately succeeded in overcoming it. Conversely,

I've seen dramatic changes in the lives of those willing to humble themselves and ask for help.

Part of the reason we don't ask for help is the belief that our sin is somehow unique, that we're the only ones who have this problem or that we are not normal because we have these struggles. Stephen Arterburn has published a great book on sexual temptation called *Every Man's Battle.*[16] What I love about that title is it reminds us that everyone struggles with lust. Not just "bad" people, not just "dirty" people—everyone. (Stephen and coauthor Shannon Ethridge have a companion volume entitled *Every Woman's Battle.*[17] Lust is by no means something only guys struggle with.)

The key to communicating this principle to your children is to share with them, in ways that are appropriate for their age, the times you have received help in fighting temptation. By saying to them, "Sometimes I go talk to a Christian counselor for help working through things," or "I know I wouldn't be able to make it in my walk with Christ if it weren't for friends I can share life with," you remove the stigma attached to asking for help. You can say to them a million times, "You can always come to me for help," but unless you model it, they aren't going to buy in.

The reward for my friend Brandon was he got his son back—the fully alive, joyful, loving son he knew was there all along. And that is what God desires for all of His sons and daughters—to become the fully alive, fully human beings He created us to be. As Jesus said, "The thief comes only to steal and kill and destroy. I came that they may have life and have it abundantly."[18]

Chapter 4

FOCUS ON WHAT YOU DON'T HAVE

The Deadly Sin of Envy

10 WAYS TO RUIN YOUR CHILD'S LIFE THROUGH ENVY

1. Look in the mirror and figure out what God made wrong about you so you can fix it.
2. Compare your children to one another so they'll know who is ahead.
3. Your strengths don't matter. Focus on where you are weak.
4. Image is everything. If you want to be a better person, spend more on your appearance.
5. Withhold attention and affection from your children unless they perform well in competition with others.
6. Find friends you can commiserate with about all the stuff you don't have yet.
7. Watch lots of advertising. It's a great source of truth.
8. Help your kids express rage when they lose a competition so they'll remember winning is everything.
9. Use social media to keep up with the Joneses.
10. God only loves perfect people, so try harder.

ADDING INCHES

Jesus had short disciples. How do I know? In his famous Sermon on the Mount, he warns them: "Therefore I tell you, do not be anxious about your life, what you will eat or what you will drink, nor about your body, what you will put on."[1] He continues, "And which of you by being anxious can add a single hour to his span of life?"[2]

That's the usual translation. However, the original text can just as well be read, "Which of you by worrying can add a single inch to his height?" Apparently, these guys were not able to pull off a slam dunk at the local basketball court, and it had them all stressed out.

Jesus tries to get them to change their focus: "And why are you anxious about clothing? Consider the lilies of the field, how they grow: they neither toil nor spin, yet I tell you, even Solomon in all his glory was not arrayed like one of these. But if God so clothes the grass of the field, which today is alive and tomorrow is thrown into the oven, will he not much more clothe you, O you of little faith?"[3]

Isn't that just what we do today? We feel insecure about our physical appearance—too short, too tall, too fat, too skinny—so we try to make up for it with fancy clothes, whether it's a boy in a hundred-dollar pair of Air Jordans or a grown man in a thousand-dollar pair of Italian leather dress shoes.

Where do we pick up these insecurities and feelings of inadequacy? For most of us, it probably started in our early-teen or even preteen years. Someone appoints himself the "pointer outer of differences."

- "Hey, did you know you have a big nose?"
- "Wow, I've never seen anyone with that many freckles."
- "Have your elbows always looked like that, or did something happen to you?"

Maybe a bully made fun of you. Maybe a parent said those terrible words to you: "Why can't you be more like your sister?" Maybe you simply noticed it yourself in the mirror one day. You were different. And try as you might, there was nothing you could do to change it.

For me, it was my teeth. Specifically, my two front teeth. They were large. They stuck straight out—so much so that I could not close my mouth without my teeth still showing. Kids called me Bucky Beaver or Bugs Bunny. I was embarrassed to smile, and it undercut my confidence.

In sixth grade I asked a cute girl to go with me to the school dance, but she turned me down. Not long after that, right near my locker, I heard her say yes to an eighth-grade football player. It didn't occur to me that she might be smitten by this older, bigger, more mature guy. I just thought, *If I didn't look like such a freak, she would have said yes to me.*

When you feel as if you don't measure up in some way, it hurts. You fear you won't be accepted or approved or respected. You feel you're not good enough. And the urge to overcome that gnawing sense of insufficiency can drive you to do some crazy things.

Here are a few ways people try to make up for inadequacy when they feel they don't measure up:

- Spending a great deal of time and money on the latest fads or fashions
- Buying cars, houses, vacations, or material items as status symbols
- Demonstrating excessive competitiveness in sports, academics, or jobs in an obsessive effort to be number one
- Devoting undue attention to looking fit, with an emphasis on appearance rather than on health
- Jockeying for a position at work, sacrificing family to climb the ladder of success
- Treating sex and relationships as a form of conquest or trophy
- Trying to be more spiritual, more religious, or more devoted than others at church, not out of love for God but to impress people

Other times, people give up the fight. Believing they can't win at the game of life, they decide it's better to intentionally fail and adopt a strategy of self-destruction. Some examples include:

- Hiding a natural appearance with hair, makeup, and clothes
- Being so quiet as to become invisible
- Deliberately failing out of school or getting fired from a job
- Using sarcasm and self-deprecating humor as a way to mask pain
- Numbing the pain of self-rejection with food, drugs, or sexual immorality

Envy is one of the root factors from which these varied outward symptoms can grow. Envy basically has two components: comparing oneself to others and looking at the outside instead of the inside. Together these two elements lead to a life focused on what a person doesn't have rather than on what God blessed him or her with on the inside. Life has glorious potential. Let's unpack those two parts a little further.

COMPARISON

I once saw a billboard for a handyman company that read We Repair the Stuff Your Husband Tried to Fix. I think they may have had me in mind. I'm not much of a do-it-yourselfer, but one thing I do know is the importance of measuring correctly. The old saying goes, "Measure twice, cut once," but if you have the wrong measuring stick, there's no way you can cut correctly. Your whole project is going to fall apart.

The apostle Paul wrote to the church of Corinth about their measuring stick: "We wouldn't dare say that we are as wonderful as these other men who tell you how important they are! But they are only comparing themselves with each other, using themselves as the standard of measurement. How ignorant!"[4]

Paul is saying a wise person never builds his or her life using other people as the measuring stick. Why not?

In the first place, comparison to other people is always relative. For example, have you ever noticed how short NBA point guards are—until you see them off the court standing next to a regular-size person? It all depends on whom you stand next to.

Even worse, by comparing ourselves with other people, we miss the opportunity to compare ourselves with God's true standard. You see, the ideal of perfection God wants us to strive for is the standard of Jesus Christ. We are told to be "building up the body of Christ, until we all attain to the unity of the faith and of the knowledge of the Son of God, to mature manhood, to the measure of the stature of the fullness of Christ"[5] and to "put on the new self, which is being renewed in knowledge after the image of its creator."[6]

The most common reason people miss a target is they don't keep their eyes on what they are aiming for in the first place. In the same way, a person obsessed with comparing himself or herself with other people is bound to miss the target of becoming more like Jesus.

Of course, I don't mean God wants you to look like a Jewish carpenter from the first century AD. When Scripture speaks of the "image of God," it's talking about His inner character, not His outer appearance. We are to allow Jesus to live in us, transforming us so we become like Him at the level of the heart—which leads us to the second element of envy, looking at the outside.

OUTSIDE IN

When we look with envy at other people, inevitably we are looking only at the surface level of their lives. Let's go back to those short disciples. In some way, they had accepted a belief that defined their worth as individuals and perhaps their masculinity in terms of their outer appearance. Our culture talks big about valuing unique individual worth, but we define femininity in terms of outward beauty or sexual attractiveness. In a hundred subtle ways we reinforce the belief that a man's worth is dictated by his size, strength, and wealth. Sometimes it seems as if the entire multibillion-dollar advertising industry is built on promoting envy.

Jesus says to His followers, "Seek first the kingdom of God and his righteousness, and all these things will be added to you." In other words, it's as if Jesus is saying, "None of that matters to me; just pursue my kingdom purpose for you, and all the rest will sort itself out." I love what a friend of mine has done: Since this verse of the Bible happens to be Matthew 6:33, she has her alarm clock set to 6:33 a.m., so God's kingdom is her first thought of every day.

Jesus is not making some naive statement that the outside doesn't matter. It does, and He knows it does. Tall people generally play basketball better than short people. That's a fact. Rich guys get more dates than broke ones. Statistically, pretty people make more money and get more promotions than the less attractive. Those are the ugly facts of life.

What Jesus *is* saying is that those things don't matter for the ultimate purpose you were created to fulfill. He has a beautiful, unique, brilliant plan for your life, and He knows what it takes to get you there. If you needed to be tall to accomplish His plan, God would have made you tall. Just seek the kingdom, and that stuff will sort itself out.

All too often the problem is, we're not seeking His kingdom; we're seeking our own little kingdom, and the way God made us seems all wrong. If your life purpose is to love God and love people, a few zits probably won't get in your way. But if your life purpose is to get other people to like and admire you, a pimple can ruin your day. The next thing you know, you're envying the gal next to you with the flawless complexion. Or the guy next to you with the perfectly straight front teeth.

WASTED POTENTIAL

The great tragedy of envy is not just that it makes us miserable when we experience it. The worst part is it robs us of our God-given potential. The boy who is a prodigious artist won't go to drawing class because he thinks his life would be better if he spent more time on sports instead. The girl who is brilliant at science majors in English because that's what some other girls she admires did. A dad works overtime to afford the big new house in the gated community and misses the opportunity to spend time with the people in the perfectly good house he already has. The mom obsessed with keeping that house looking like a magazine cover misses the joy of making messes with her little ones.

God gives us these gifts, these precious treasures, every single day, but we often miss them because we are busy looking for something else. I know it saddens me when I see my children miss opportunities, so it must truly grieve the heart of God when we do, for He alone knows how many gifts we have thrown in the trash.[7]

One way I have tried to help my children combat envy is by giving them specific praise about their strengths, tied directly back to God's purpose. For example, my son was given a rainbow loom used to weave colorful rubber bands together into bracelets or other creations. Some of the patterns involved are quite complex, but PW took the initiative to get on YouTube, watch some tutorial videos other kids had created, and figure out for himself how to make the designs. I didn't just say to him vaguely, "Good job." I told him specifically, "I'm proud of you for figuring that out. You showed a lot of resourcefulness and ingenuity." Then I asked him, "Do you know what that means? God can use people like you to figure stuff out."

We went on to talk for a while about how there are complex problems in the world—poor communities and nations, diseases and wars—and that the same character qualities PW used with his rainbow loom were qualities God could use to solve bigger problems in His world. I don't want my son to see the gifts of others and feel envy; I want him to know he has gifts, and those gifts matter to the purposes of God in the world.

It was a little harder for me when my daughter Kaylee took up swimming. She worked hard and practiced every day with her swim team, but she wasn't particularly good at it. In fact, she often came in last. But it didn't seem to faze her. After a race she would cheerfully hop out of the water, walk over, and congratulate the winner. I have to be honest: The competitive-sports guy inside of me was thinking, *You're not supposed to congratulate the winner. You're supposed to hate her and vow to beat her next time!*

However, I learned two lessons from my daughter's lack of envy. First, she wasn't running her race—literally. Kaylee loves *The Little Mermaid,* and like Ariel in the story, my daughter needed to find her legs. The water wasn't her thing, but she's incredible on land. If she had obsessed about winning at swimming, she might never have discovered her talent for running and might never have been more than a mediocre swimmer.

Second, and more important, I saw that my daughter has a gift for making friends. Her ease of going over to the winner and congratulating her on a win was a mark of someone who is really good at building relationships. As a pastor's daughter, Kaylee gets placed in a wide variety of social situations with all kinds of people. Time and time again, I've seen how she is gifted at adapting to people wherever she finds herself. I know that is an ability God can use greatly to build His kingdom. That's something Mr. Competitive-Sports Guy would never be able to appreciate, but it's far more valuable in the long run.

THE POWER OF ACCEPTANCE

These steps are useful but, once again, the best way to avoid ruining your child with envy is to deal with envy in yourself. And the critical step in that battle may be to accept the way God designed you. As Pastor Andy Stanley says, acceptance fuels influence.[8] You can't influence your kids if you can't accept them, and you can't fully accept others until you have accepted yourself.

After all those years of being called Bugs Bunny, I finally got my teeth fixed. They are now, by the grace of God and the skill of a great orthodontist, as neat and straight as they can be—and they fit inside my mouth. But every time I smile I am reminded of the self-rejection I felt as a boy. Instead of reliving the pain, though, I choose to use it as a reminder of how much God loves and accepts me, even with my self-proclaimed imperfections. And I try to use it as a reminder to be sensitive toward the self-rejection others may be feeling, motivating me to share God's love and grace with them.

So I'm grateful for crooked teeth. I guess you could say my being a Bugs Bunny look-alike taught me how to overcome envy.

What about you? Are you grateful for the "crooked teeth" in your life, or are they driving you to envy others? I've named some of the crazy things people are driven to do when they don't feel worthy or adequate, and maybe you recognized yourself in that list. Maybe you know it's time to deal with the root of self-rejection that is driving your life down the path of envy and threatening to destroy your children with you.

Here's what I want you to do: make a list of your unchangeable features, the facts about how God designed you. Your parents (or lack thereof), your brothers and sisters, your birth order. Your physical appearance. Your racial and ethnic background. Your aptitudes and abilities. Your skills and talents. The educational, financial, and social opportunities given to you. Can you look at yourself in the mirror and agree with God that His creation is "very good"?[9] If not, go back and put a star next to all the items on your list you have struggled to accept.

Next, add to your list the scars that have come into your life. Things people did to you causing you hurt or shame. Accidents that happened. Defects caused by genetics or disease that hinder you. People who let you down, neglected you, or didn't show you the love you needed. God didn't cause these things directly, but He did allow them. If you feel these scars make you inadequate, dirty, spoiled, or unworthy, write them down.

Now take some time to reflect on God's greatness and God's goodness. Do you really believe God is love?[10] Do you believe you have a wise, sovereign, all-powerful Creator? Do you believe God "causes all things to work together for good to those who love God, to those who are called according to His purpose"?[11]

When you are ready, pray this prayer by faith:

Father, thank You for creating me just as I am. You have called what You created very good, and by faith I accept Your evaluation of me, even when it does not seem good in my eyes. Forgive me for rejecting the way You made me. Forgive me for envying others whom I thought were better than I or had more of the good things in life than I do. I know You have already given me everything I need for my present happiness in Christ Jesus. Thank You even for the scars that have come into my life, because I know that while others may have intended them for evil, You intended them for good. What You have allowed into my life, You will turn into something beautiful in Your good time. I commit myself anew to live for You, to seek first Your kingdom, and to pursue wholeheartedly the purpose for which You made me. When I am tempted to envy others, remind me of this prayer, and of Your love for me. I ask this in Jesus's name. Amen.

Get Practical: Eight Unenvious Steps

So how do we avoid allowing envy to ruin our lives and the lives of our children? Here are eight steps you can try.

1. Be careful what you wish for.

One powerful phrase a parent must be extra cautious with is "I wish I were …" Children learn to wish for what you wish for. If you wish to be like others who are richer or thinner or more happily married, your children will learn to envy. On the other hand, if you wish to be like Christ, to find ways to share God's love and solve the world's problems, they will learn to seek the kingdom of God. Once you've set the example, you'll be ready to help your children work through it when they say things like "I wish I were like so-and-so." Help them uncover why they wish that, and whether or not that wish is compatible with God's purpose for their lives.

2. Compare with care.

The phrase "I wish you were like so-and-so" is almost always destructive. It conveys that a child is not loved and accepted for who he or she is. Unlike challenging goals and clear steps of action, wishes are vague and not actionable, so they crush the spirit. Examples can be used to inspire, if you allow for personalization. Inspiring is, "Abraham Lincoln taught himself law by reading at home. I believe you can accomplish great things, too, if you continue to work hard practicing your reading." Saying, "Beethoven wrote his first symphony at age seven; why can't you even play 'Mary Had a Little Lamb'?" is not.

3. Deconstruct advertising.

I said earlier that the advertising industry seems to be built on envy, but that's not entirely true. Advertising can be beneficial and informative, but the key is to become a savvy ad consumer. Talk to your

children about the process. "Someone made this ad. They intentionally chose pictures of children who look excited and happy about
playing with that toy. They are trying to convince you to buy it. It
may not really be that cool." Pulling back the curtain on the process
builds your child's envy immunity. (One great way to do this is to
have your kids actually create some ads for products, so they think
through the selling process.)

4. Celebrate others' good fortunes.

Teach your children by word and example to "rejoice with those
who rejoice."[12] If a friend gets a new toy, a new car, the latest tech
gadget, a promotion at work, don't say, "Why couldn't I get that?"
The world is not a zero-sum game where one person winning always
means someone else is losing. Instead say, "That's great! I'm happy
for them!" Celebrating someone else's win kills envy at the root.

5. Walk away from "envytations."

Ever noticed how people love to invite you to envy with them?
People like to commiserate on how bad they have it and how unfair life is. Don't accept that invitation. Change the subject or walk
away. Remember the wisdom of Proverbs: "A tranquil heart gives
life to the flesh, but envy makes the bones rot."[13]

6. Praise character, not performance.

Children learn what is important to you by what you praise. If you
want them to learn to look at the heart and not focus on surface
appearances, teach them by going below the surface of actions.
Instead of saying, "I'm proud of you for getting a good grade on

your test," say, "I'm proud of you for listening to your teacher and studying hard. That shows the character qualities of attentiveness and diligence. It really shows in your grade." Instead of saying, "Jill is such a pretty girl," try saying, "Jill has a joyful spirit. I can tell by the way she always smiles. Her heart really lights up her face in a beautiful way." That way your children will be inspired to emulate good character rather than learning to envy surface behaviors.

7. Point to a bigger mission.

If your child's world consists only of doing things for themselves, envy is almost inevitable. However, if you expose them to opportunities to serve the poor and needy, talk to them about God's purpose for the world, and take them with you on a mission, they begin to get a glimpse of what it means for God's kingdom to come on earth as it is in heaven. Say things like, "God put our family together to make a difference for Him in the world," or "I knew from the day you were born that God had a special plan to use you to bless the whole world." As they get caught up the beauty of God's vision, envy will fade out of sight.

8. Be a strengths finder.

Marcus Buckingham and Donald O. Clifton wrote a self-help book called *Now, Discover Your Strengths*[14] that has challenged the business world to think less about fixing weaknesses and more about maximizing strengths. The old adage was, "Be a well-rounded person." But think about it this way: If God made you a spoon, it's great to be well rounded. But if He made you a knife or a fork, what you want is to get sharper or pointier. Our natural tendency is to think we can improve our children by criticizing their weaknesses, but generally, we can accomplish more by helping them discover and develop their strengths.

Here is the beautiful thing. When you accept God's love and purpose for yourself, you will reflect that love and acceptance with your children. When that happens, their hearts will no longer be fertile soil for weeds of envy. Instead, they will be ready to receive the seed of God's truth and bear incredible fruit for His kingdom as they develop and utilize the unique gifts and embrace the calling He has given to each one of them.

Chapter 5

IT'S ALL ABOUT ME

The Deadly Sin of Greed

10 WAYS TO RUIN YOUR CHILD'S LIFE THROUGH GREED

1. More is always better.
2. A great parent is one who gives his or her kids every single thing they want.
3. If you have to give, let everyone know what a sacrifice it is.
4. Talk to your kids about how evil rich people are. Rich means anyone with more than you.
5. Don't assign toys to your kids; let them fight it out to see who gets them, to prepare for the real world.
6. If there's a lag in the conversation, talk about yourself.
7. Avoid exposing your kids to poor people. That's just sad.
8. Save way more than you need for retirement. Real life starts then.
9. Given the choice, always work more hours instead of spending more time with your children. Think of how much happier they will be with all the extra stuff you'll be able to buy for them.
10. Avoid new relationships. They always cost time and money.

BECOMING SCROOGE

It's Christmastime as I write, and the Alabama Shakespeare Festival in our town is once again producing *A Christmas Carol*. It is a story that has been reworked a dozen ways, from TV specials to feature-length films. No doubt the enduring popularity of Charles Dickens's classic is partly due to the nostalgia and tradition we associate with the holiday season. But beyond that, I think our society has a fascination with this story because we sense we are all in danger of becoming a Scrooge. We are fascinated by his psychology and want to know how a person can become so consumed by greed that he forgets how to love. And more important, how can such a person be redeemed?

We may think we are immune to greed. After all, not many of us sit around in countinghouses with stacks of gold pieces, snarling, "Bah, humbug!" at Christmas well-wishers. It's those CEOs and the corrupt politicians and the one percent who have greed issues. But in truth, we don't need to reach the extreme caricature of Ebenezer Scrooge for greed to get its hands on us. In fact, greed can take many forms, some of which have nothing to do with money—and it can infect anyone, rich or poor, old or young.

In a word, greed is not about the money; it's about the "me."

WHY DOES IT HAVE TO BE SO HARD?

In one of Jesus's most radical teaching moments, He told His disciples to put their "me" to death. He challenged them:

> If anyone would come after me, let him deny himself and take up his cross and follow me. For whoever would save his life will lose it, but whoever loses his life for my sake and the gospel's will save it. For what does it profit a man to gain the whole world and forfeit his soul? For what can a man give in return for his soul?[1]

We tend to think of the word *soul* as synonymous with spirit, but the Greek word for soul is *psyche*, as in psychology. It could perhaps be better translated your *self*. Jesus is saying, in order to find yourself, you have to lose yourself. Greed doesn't pay, because the more stuff you get—even if you get the whole world—the more you lose yourself, your humanity, your God-given identity.

My younger daughter, Cate, recently had an encounter with what Jesus calls "taking up your cross," even at age six. We had taken our second foster placement, a little boy I'll call Riley. Our first placement had been a baby when we brought him home, and Cate loved helping Mom take care of him. But this was a new challenge: this was someone old enough to take Cate's toys, invade her space, and interfere with her life. As the youngest of three, Cate wasn't used to having to accommodate others; she was usually the one being accommodated. And Riley was upsetting that balance.

In particular, he liked Cate's red bouncy ball. After several clashes over Riley playing with her ball, Cate asked, "Can't Riley just go home now?"

Rachael sat down with her and explained, "Riley doesn't have a home. If he doesn't stay with us, he doesn't have anywhere to go." She went on to ask, "Don't you think you should share your ball with Riley? Do you know what Jesus would want you to do?" Cate thought for a moment and sighed, looking at the ball. "I know, Mom," she answered. "But why does it have to be so hard?"

Isn't that what all of us want to say at some point? "Jesus, I know what You say; I know what it means to follow You. But why does it have to be so hard? Why does it have to feel like taking up a cross?"

To answer that question for Cate and for ourselves, let's think a little more about Cate's relationship with that red ball. Cate could sit in a room by herself for hours and play with that ball, and there would be absolutely nothing wrong with that. Loving the ball is not the essence of greed. Like many children, Cate can actually be quite generous. It would not be uncommon for her to see another child who looked sad and offer to share a toy with him or her. She is capable of seeing others and empathizing with them, and that empathy moves her quite naturally to give.

But in this situation, that natural desire to give ran dry. Why? Because she was looking at the ball and not at the boy. When her love for the ball became the focus of her perception, she was no longer seeing Riley. And without seeing him as a person, there was nothing to trigger her sense of empathy. She could still share with him out of a sense of obligation (or because she was afraid of getting into trouble), but it felt really hard.

God is not some cosmic killjoy who hates you and wants you to hate yourself. When Jesus says to take up your cross and lose yourself, it's not that He wants you to suffer. On the contrary, it is because He understands that, at the deepest level, your humanity, your identity, your true self can only come to life in relationships with other people. When you lose your life, you will find it—in the process of creating the bonds of relationship with others. But nothing hinders those relationships from forming or blinds you to the humanness of others more than greed.

DESPISING AND DEHUMANIZING

Cate's story demonstrates that while greed appears to be a problem with materialism or making things too important, at heart it is really a people problem. Listen with new ears to what Jesus said about money: "No one can serve two masters, for either he will hate the one and love the other, or he will be devoted to the one and despise the other. You cannot serve God and money."[2]

Why can't you serve both God and money? Not because there isn't room in your life for two important things. We do that all the time, balancing multiple priorities. No, Jesus says you can't serve both God and money because loving one will change your perception of the other. When you love money, you will start to hate God. So of course you won't serve Him; He won't seem worth it to you. You'll hardly notice He's there. That's what it means to despise someone: to treat the person as if he or she isn't even worth noticing. If greed is powerful enough to make us despise God, it is certainly enough to make us despise other mere mortals.

Here's how it works. To begin with, we have the ability to see people as people, to respond to their needs, hopes, and fears as if they were our own. Greed, however, says, "Only focus on your own needs and wants, your own hopes and fears." To do that, we have to shut other people out. We only see the ball, not the boy. People become objects to us—either tools we can use or obstacles to be moved out of our way, but certainly not human beings. And when we stop treating others as human, we stop being human ourselves. As Henri Nouwen wrote, "Every time I take a step in the direction of generosity, I know that I am moving from fear to love."[3]

The writers of Disney's animated movie *Tangled* got this message dead-on in their characterization of the villain. Mother Gothel constantly warns Rapunzel to guard the power of her magical hair from others. "The world is dark and selfish and cruel," she proclaims. "If it finds even the slightest ray of sunshine, it destroys it!" Of course, this is exactly what Gothel has done herself, kidnapping Rapunzel as a baby and keeping her locked up in a tower. What she fears in others is really a reflection of what is in her own heart. Her most ironic line in the film is, "Great. Now I'm the bad guy." The audience can see what she can't see of herself: By making everyone else out to be a monster, she has become a monster herself. By dehumanizing others, she has lost her own humanity.

Greed is another form of idolatry, and the Scriptures warn that those who idolize silver and gold eventually become just as inhuman as those cold, lifeless metals. In the poetry of the Bible we find this image:

Their idols are silver and gold,
    the work of human hands.
They have mouths, but do not speak;
    eyes, but do not see.
They have ears, but do not hear;
    noses, but do not smell.
They have hands, but do not feel;
    feet, but do not walk;
    and they do not make a sound in their throat.
Those who make them become like them;
    so do all who trust in them.[4]

"I WILL HAVE NOTHING"

The unspoken fear that grips us when we begin to think about greed versus giving is the belief that we need just a little greed to protect us from the greed of others. We fear that if our hearts are too soft, people will use and abuse us as if we were doormats. In fact, the opposite is true: people whose hearts have the greatest empathy and compassion are the most able to set healthy boundaries.

One day my cowriter, Ken Roach, found his daughter Abbie sitting alone in her room crying. When he asked what was wrong, she explained, "One day I will come into my room, and it will be completely empty. Drew [her younger brother] will take everything I have, and I will have nothing left."

Abbie was putting into plain words what most of us feel at some point: That it's all well and good to talk about giving and generosity, but at some point we've got to look out for number one. If we don't stand up for our own interests, we'll end up with nothing. That's just common sense, right?

Yet, in walks Jesus and says, "Give to everyone who begs from you, and from one who takes away your goods do not demand them back. And as you wish that others would do to you, do so to them."[5]

So is Jesus taking the side of the little brothers of the world who want to come and take all of our toys until we having nothing left to play with? Is He telling us we have to be doormats and allow others to abuse us? Not at all. Remember, even the Golden Rule has a boundary—do unto others as you would have others do to you. Jesus is saying, change your perception. See the other person as an equal, a human being just like yourself, with feelings and needs just like yours.

Treating others as you would have them treat you doesn't always mean giving stuff away. Sometimes it simply means giving time, attention, or respect. People need to be seen and heard and valued. Jesus says that's what you want for yourself; now go and treat others the same way.

Ken would tell you that on most days Abbie has more fun playing with her little brother than she does with any of her toys. They can laugh until they cry and play together for hours. In these moments it's not that Abbie is trying hard to be good, forcing herself to like her brother because Jesus said to. She's not thinking about it at all. She is simply seeing him as a person and responding to him naturally, with her God-given ability to love and enjoy being with him. She is looking at the boy, not the ball. And in losing her life, she is finding it.

Ultimately, when we learn to overcome greed and teach our children to do the same, we aren't just putting the self-centered, me-focused ego on the cross; we are allowing our true selves—the generous, kind, free persons God created us to be—to come to life within us. As Jesus said, when you lose yourself, you find yourself. And there's no greater joy than getting to be there and observe when our children find their true selves.

Get Practical: Three Greed Busters

So how do we, as parents, lead our children to avoid the trap of greed? How do we enable them to find their true self in loving, mutually giving relationships with others rather than a selfish focus on me, me, me? Here are three helpful keys.

1. Use the gift of siblings.

First, understand the dynamics of relationships between brothers and sisters. God has designed the family to be a staging ground where we can form a template for how we will forge all future relationships. It's not surprising that Scripture uses the language of siblings to explain what it means in practice to love God: "If anyone says, 'I love God,' and hates his brother, he is a liar; for he who does not love his brother whom he has seen cannot love God whom he has not seen."[6]

Siblings in the Bible don't have a great track record. The first murder occurred in the first family when Cain killed Abel. Ishmael despised Isaac. Jacob cheated Esau. Joseph's brothers sold him into slavery. If nothing else, we get the message that God understands it's hard to love your brother (or sister).

On the other hand, we are told that the ultimate example of love comes from a brother. Jesus sacrificed Himself for us, so that He might become to us "the firstborn among many brothers."[7]

To leverage the power of that relationship, we parents need to recognize the differences in birth order. We don't live in a culture with rigid rules giving special rights to the firstborn as in ancient Israel (and most other societies in history), but there are still some general principles at work. The psychology is evident: the first child comes into a world where he or she is the sole focus of Mom and Dad, while subsequent children come into a world where they are never alone.

In a nutshell, the result is that a firstborn boy or girl tends to have a greater response to authority (whether very obedient or very disobedient, rule follower or rebel), while the second-born boy or girl tends to have a greater response to peers (seeking acceptance and approval from others, whether through competition or cooperation). To put it another way, the eldest has the choice to be either just like his or her parents or the opposite of them. The second has the choice to be either just like the older sibling or the opposite of him or her.

That summary is of course greatly oversimplified, but it draws attention to how parents should go about solving problems. When the second born is misbehaving, often the solution is to work on the relationship with the older brother or sister. When you can enlist the older child's help in modeling and motivating a younger sibling, you help train the older one to think like a leader, and you may have more success in influencing younger ones.

In contrast, when an older child is misbehaving, it is often a signal that you need to work more on your relationship with that child. Every child needs one-on-one time with Mom and Dad, but firstborn children especially need some solo time, both to reinforce your love and support for them and to give them a break from the pressure of being the leader all the time.

I'm grateful that one of my mentors modeled for me the practice of having breakfast with each of my children every week. That "daddy date" is a great time to assess how things are going and to give each of my children some one-on-one attention, love, and affection. That bond, in turn, gives me a better foundation to build on when I need to help them through a conflict with a brother or sister. By creating a safe space for conversation, I am able to impart wisdom into their lives.

The point of all this, remember, is to help your children learn to see others as people; to empathize with one another's hurts and needs; to resist the temptation of greed that would lead them to despise or dehumanize one another. It's amazing how a child who is relatively polite to others, obedient to teachers, and kind to friends, can suddenly turn around and treat a brother or sister like dirt. But that just goes to show how deep the roots of sin and greed can run. As messy as the relationship between brothers and sisters can be, it is God's best gift to us to help eradicate the weed of greed.

Which brings up a note for those of you who are parenting an only child. I'm not telling you your child is doomed to be greedy because he or she doesn't have any siblings to practice generosity with. However, I do think you should be intentional about putting your child in situations with other children where he or she has to practice give-and-take. It's especially valuable to put single children in environments where they have to deal with children younger than themselves. Volunteer together in your church's children's ministry, or coach a team and make your child your assistant coach. You will stretch his or her leadership muscles and provide opportunities to practice focusing on someone other than me, me, me.

2. Don't make your home a commune.

At the beginning of the chapter, I made the point that greed is not about the money; it's about the "me." However, money and material possessions are certainly a primary way we work out how to live a life of generosity and love. Some people draw the conclusion from this that the best way to teach their family to share is to practice the idea that no one owns anything—everything belongs to the whole family. In essence, they live in a commune.

The problem with that thinking is that without personal ownership, there's no personal giving. What's mine I can choose to keep, share, or give away. What's *ours* can't be hoarded, but it can't be given away either. Often the result is that greed simply becomes more subtle. Children may not argue about what's "mine," but they still argue about when it's "my turn" or how much is "my share."

Look at how the Scriptures teach us to deal with the greedy attitude of a thief. Paul writes to the early Christians in Ephesus, "Let the thief no longer steal, but rather let him labor, doing honest work with his own hands, so that he may have something to share with anyone in need."[8] Notice the progression. First, he takes for himself what belongs to others. Second, he learns to work so that he will have his own possessions. Third, he gives away those possessions to others. This is true victory over greed. Without the second step—acquiring things for oneself through honest work—the third step of giving would not have the same meaning.

Each family needs to work out the details of how this works in practice, but I would encourage you to have some things that belong to everyone—family resources, that all must learn how to share—and other things that belong individually to each child. These things they choose when to share and when not to share or when to give away, so they have the opportunity to practice true giving as well as how to set healthy boundaries.

Likewise, creating opportunities for children to work for money as they grow older has a triple benefit: it trains them to develop a work ethic, teaches them how to handle money, and gives them the opportunity to learn to give. Very young children may benefit from having money given to them to give to others, but the older children get, the more they need to work for that money in order for the giving to have any real meaning.

John Wesley, cofounder of the Methodist church, had a saying about money: "Earn all you can, save all you can, give all you can." We might have expected a preacher to tell us to "give all you can," but what makes Wesley's teaching profound is he recognized it is only through earning and saving that we are really in a position to do the giving. Wise parents create opportunities for their children to earn and save so they can also give, knowing that giving is what breaks the hold of greed.

3. Change your shoes.

The saying goes, "Don't judge someone's life until you walk a mile in his shoes." In other words, you have to know someone's story to understand his or her actions and attitudes. Empathy, not sympathy, is the opposite of greed. Sympathy says, "I feel sorry for you." It can show kindness, but it can also be just as dehumanizing as selfishness if we treat the person we give to as merely a project to work on or a problem to solve. Empathy, on the other hand, says, "I feel what you feel, because I can identify with you." It requires the skill of finding common ground, regardless of how different the other person may appear to be on the surface. Thus, empathy depends on storytelling. We want our children to become expert story collectors.

Jessica Jackley, founder of the nonprofit microfinance organization Kiva, demonstrates how powerful storytelling can be. Kiva has assisted with funding literally billions of dollars in zero-interest loans to entrepreneurs in developing countries, having an unprecedented impact on the lives of the poor. Yet Jessica reports that as a young person, she wanted nothing to do with poverty. Like many churchgoers, she was inundated as a child with images from missionaries of sick and starving children, the extreme needs of the poor. In time she was overwhelmed by the need and, not feeling she could ever do anything about it, she blocked it out. Emotionally, she simply couldn't afford to think about the poor.

That all changed when she went as a journalism student to actually interview a group of poor people in Africa. As she helped to document their stories, she discovered they were real people. Yes, their needs were great, but they could also smile, laugh, tell a joke, think for themselves, and come up with ideas and plans to improve their situation. Jessica built Kiva around that simple experience of storytelling. Visitors to Kiva's website aren't asked to give a gift but to make a zero-interest loan. Even better, they don't give to a nameless, faceless need. Every Kiva donor sees a picture and reads the story of the person they are making their loan to. They are entering into a partnership with a person, not a transaction with a need.[9]

What's the point for parents? Very simply, we need to teach our children to seek out the stories of others. You can start this when they are young by discussing the characters they watch on TV or in movies. Ask questions that encourage empathy:

- "How do you think that made her feel?"
- "Why do you think he did that?"
- "What do you think they were thinking about when they did that?"

As your children grow older, begin to ask those questions about real world events and people, whether it's a lesson in their history class, something they see on the news, or a new person they meet at school. Imagining what it would be like to be a slave in 1840, a German Jew in 1940, or a refugee in modern-day Syria broadens perspective on the world in a way that purely intellectual learning does not. It moves a person from fact finder to story collector.

Many children (and many adults) lack the conversational skills to uncover the stories of others. We're much better at talking about ourselves or our interests. To start with, they need very specific training on what to say: "When you meet someone for the first time, tell them your name, and ask them what their name is. Ask them where they are from, what their family is like, or what they like to do." Later they can learn to ask follow-up questions.

If your child likes sports and he meets another child who likes sports, the conversation may flow easily, but if he meets someone who has different interests, he might need help knowing how to explore that. Role-play on how to say things such as, "Oh, you like photography? I've never tried that. What other things do you like to do? What do you like about doing them?"

Jesus demonstrated this kind of skill. When he saw Zacchaeus up in a tree, he wanted to have lunch with him. He paid attention to Zacchaeus's story when others did not. As a result, that story was radically changed. Zacchaeus went from stealing people's money to giving his wealth away. Jesus turned common ground into higher ground.

As parents, we can model story collecting and finding common ground. Invite people into your home for a shared meal, and ask them to share their experiences. Never speak about people or groups of people in ways that demean, demonize, and dehumanize them, even if you strongly disagree with them on some issue. Take time to listen to your children's own stories, even when you are tired or angry or busy. That can be the hardest but also the most rewarding way to teach your children empathy by example.

Becoming a story collector is a fundamental way to fulfill the Golden Rule. We all have a deep need to share our story, to be seen and heard and valued for who we are. When we give that gift to others, we honor them, and in doing so we enrich our own story. Along the way, we take the focus off of the "me" and cut off the weed of greed at the root. When we listen to the stories of others, we are looking at the boy, not the ball.

Cate frequently goes into Riley's room at night to snuggle with him, share some of her stuffed animals, and help him go to sleep.

We have a baby monitor that stays on in his room, and not too long ago we overheard Cate in there with him. Copying a bedtime ritual Rachael began long ago with our children, Cate was singing "Jesus Loves Me" to Riley and substituting his name into the song. "Yes, Jesus loves Riley; yes, Jesus loves Riley; the Bible tells me so."

In that moment, greed lost its grip. In losing her life, Cate was finding it. By sharing the love of Jesus with her foster brother, she was also discovering the depths of how much God loves her. And yes, as Mom and Dad listening in via the baby monitor, we shed a few tears.

What an awesome privilege it is as parents to witness God at work in our children's hearts.

Chapter 6

YOU ALWAYS NEED MORE!

The Deadly Sin of Gluttony

10 WAYS TO RUIN YOUR CHILD'S LIFE THROUGH GLUTTONY

1. Never be satisfied.
2. If a little doesn't make you happy, you just need more.
3. Religion is all about getting to heaven. That spiritual stuff doesn't help here on earth.
4. Go, go, go, 24-7. Maximizing your time is how you win.
5. Don't let church keep you from experiencing more in life. Sunday is just another day.
6. Fasting is a waste of time. What possible good could come from telling your appetites "no"?
7. Let your children dictate their own schedules for eating and sleeping, and they'll be happy.
8. It's a high-tech world. Prepare your kids for it with unlimited screen time.
9. Keep your eyes on your phone when spending time with your kids so they can see your commitment to work.
10. God never wants you to go without. If you have enough faith, you'll get whatever you want right away.

NUMBER 15

In my state of Alabama, college football is king. It's hard for people who live outside the area to comprehend how much time, energy, and emotion are spent on football here, principally on the two rival schools of Auburn University and the University of Alabama. So when the Alabama Crimson Tide won their fourteenth national championship a few years back, it was not surprising that a flood of fan merchandise followed—T-shirts, caps, bumper stickers, and other logo-inscribed items. What may be surprising to those who don't understand Alabama football fans is that the number printed on that merchandise was not 14, signifying their fourteenth championship, it was 15. That's right. As soon as Crimson Tide won, their fans were ready for another one. Even Alabama's stoic head coach Nick Saban was heard complaining that fans didn't seem to be capable of just enjoying the win. They always needed more.

The oil baron and billionaire John D. Rockefeller was once asked, "How much money is enough?" and he answered, "Just a little bit more." That *more* is the essence of gluttony, a medieval-sounding word we don't use a lot these days. Perhaps we need to bring it back, though, for it sums up so much of what is wrong in our culture. We're never satisfied. We never seem to have enough. Despite living in the midst of historically unprecedented prosperity (even given recent recessions), we always seem to be hungry for more. And more.

Gluttony is related to lust, envy, and greed. Lust looks at the future yet wants it *now*. Envy compares itself to others and wants to be *better*. And greed, as we've just seen, looks at what it has and wants it all for *me*. However, gluttony brings its own special emphasis: sheer quantity. How much do I have? How much can I get? How can I get more? *More, more, more!*

Parents have certainly been made more aware of gluttony as an issue because of the soaring rate of childhood obesity in the United States. Just as lust is typically related to sexuality and greed to money, gluttony has most often been associated with food and drink. The Centers for Disease Control and Prevention estimates that childhood obesity has doubled in the last thirty years and adolescent obesity has tripled during the same time, so more than a third of Americans under age eighteen are now considered medically overweight.[1] Of course, part of the health issue surrounding obesity has less to do with how much we eat and more to do with changes in our diet—we eat out more, eat more processed foods, and have more sedentary lifestyles.

My point is not that overweight kids are more sinful than others. The real threat of gluttony is not something you can weigh on a scale. As the saying goes, It's not what we're eating—it's what's eating us.

THE WOLF INSIDE

It's easy to caricature the glutton as a big, fat pig—the person who takes too much enjoyment in food and drink, cake and doughnuts, beer and wine. If we have to pick an animal, though, the better image for gluttony is a gaunt, starving wolf. Deep inside our psyche he haunts us—always hungry, never full, always on the hunt. The real mark of gluttony is not that we enjoy the good things in life too much, but that we enjoy them too little—in fact, in the full grip of gluttony, we lack the capacity to enjoy them at all. We are driven to find more and more because we have lost the ability to find pleasure in what we already have. In the words of the Rolling Stones, we can't get no satisfaction.

One form of glutton today is the shopping glutton. We have turned shopping into an art form. It's not about the product; it's about the process. We just love to spend money. Whole websites are dedicated to showing off your latest purchases. People take shopping vacations just so they can go somewhere new in the world and spend money. We run up our credit-card debt because we find it stress relieving to go shopping—until the bills come in, which causes more stress, which leads to more shopping.

Another modern manifestation of gluttony is the experience glutton. We constantly need new sources of excitement, new thrills. Our kids have gaming systems capable of creating incredible worlds of computer graphics that could be explored for months, but they always have to have the latest game just as soon as they burn through the levels of the last one. Others go rock climbing or whitewater rafting or skydiving in search of adventure, and each experience must be more extreme than the last for us to feel alive.

Gluttony is not just confined to the world of entertainment. We carry it right into the boardroom when we become the success glutton—craving more growth, more profits, and the latest promotion without being able to enjoy what we have already achieved. Pastor and leadership guru Bill Hybels calls this "up and to the right syndrome," picturing a graph chart showing the growth and profits of an organization; we're not happy unless that arrow is always going up, up, up as it progresses to the right.[2] Even pastors, he says, succumb to this. Pastors want a church that is growing bigger and bigger—not to reach more people with the gospel of Jesus Christ, but so our egos can feel validated.

It's no wonder, when parents are slaves to this syndrome at work, that we transfer this to our children who never feel satisfied with their accomplishments in school, in the arts, or on the ball field. Who cares about 14? We want 15.

In the blockbuster movie *Pirates of the Caribbean*, the pirate captain Barbossa gives a speech that sums up gluttony well. Having stolen cursed gold, the crew of the *Black Pearl* has been given immortality; however, it comes at the cost of being the living dead, literally walking skeletons, their senses dulled. Barbossa laments, "For too long I've been parched of thirst and unable to quench it. Too long I've been starving to death and haven't died. I feel nothing. Not the wind on my face nor the spray of the sea nor the warmth of a woman's flesh." Perhaps more of us have stolen that cursed gold than we realize.

BLESSED BY LESS

Into our world of more, more, more, Jesus's concept of who is truly blessed comes as a bit of a shock: "Blessed are you who are poor, for yours is the kingdom of God. Blessed are you who are hungry now, for you shall be satisfied. Blessed are you who weep now, for you shall laugh."[3]

Blessed (in Greek, *makarios*) is difficult to translate into one word in English. It carries the ideas of happiness, contentment, satisfaction, and inner peace, along with wealth, abundance, and prosperity. In Hebrew it would have been *shalom*.

In the famous "show me the money" scene in the movie *Jerry Maguire*, Cuba Gooding Jr.'s character calls it "the *kwan*—love, respect, community, and the dollars too; the package." Even our secular culture recognizes that blessing is about more than the money. And here is Jesus, saying that happiness, *shalom*, or *kwan* comes to those who are poor, hungry, and crying. What's up with that?

Perhaps, in part, Jesus is saying that those who lack material things have greater faith in spiritual things. And perhaps to some degree He is also saying that those who have less in the present life will have more in the next life. However, it is possible to overspiritualize Jesus's meaning. The Bible does not make the harsh divisions between the spiritual and the physical realms that we tend to make in modern times. Part of the message of Jesus is that God's realm of heaven is constantly breaking through into man's realm of earth, right here and right now. We are taught in Scripture to "set your minds on things that are above, not on things that are on earth,"[4] but we are also taught to pray, "Your kingdom come, your will be done, on earth as it is in heaven."[5] As the psalmist said of God, "The heavens are yours; the earth also is yours; the world and all that is in it, you have founded them," and, "Be exalted, O God, above the heavens! Let your glory be over all the earth!"[6]

Heaven is not "someday by and by when I die." Eternal life begins now for the follower of Jesus. The riches, the satisfaction, and the joy of the kingdom are available to us here and now, but they are only to be grasped through the process of experiencing poverty, hunger, and tears.

Consider the apostle Paul's experience with the mysterious "thorn ... in the flesh" related to us in the New Testament. We don't know exactly what it was, but it wasn't fun. He calls it "a messenger of Satan to harass me, to keep me from becoming conceited." He then goes on to say: "Three times I pleaded with the Lord about this, that it should leave me. But he said to me, 'My grace is sufficient for you, for my power is made perfect in weakness.' Therefore I will boast all the more gladly of my weaknesses, so that the power of Christ may rest upon me. For the sake of Christ, then, I am content with weaknesses, insults, hardships, persecutions, and calamities. For when I am weak, then I am strong."[7]

The extraordinary power of God on Paul's life, his role in spreading the gospel across the Roman world, and the overwhelming joy that came into his life, Paul attributes to an experience of hardship, struggle, and weakness so painful he pleaded with God to remove it.

In fact, this is not only how God dealt with Paul, but it is His pattern of dealing with people throughout the Scriptures:

- Abraham has a vision to be a great nation, but he is barren well into old age, when a child is miraculously born.

- Joseph has a dream he will be a great leader, but he endures years in slavery and in prison before God exalts him to rule over the nation of Egypt.
- Ruth loses her husband and becomes impoverished as a widow, but she finds redemption in the love of Boaz and eventually becomes the grandmother of the royal line of Israel.
- David is anointed king, but he must flee for his life from Saul into the desert until he is eventually crowned.
- Esther is an orphan who finds her people in exile, but God raises her into the position of queen so she can rescue an entire race from annihilation.
- Daniel is given wisdom to announce God's power over pagan rulers, but he and his friends are cast into a lions' den and a fiery furnace before those rulers acknowledge the truth.

Many more examples could be given. Of course, the greatest example of joy through the path of suffering is Jesus himself, of whom Paul writes:

> Have this mind among yourselves, which is yours in Christ Jesus, who, though he was in the form of God, did not count equality with God a thing to be grasped, but emptied himself, by taking the form of a servant, being born in the likeness of men. And being found in human form, he

humbled himself by becoming obedient to the
point of death, even death on a cross. Therefore
God has highly exalted him and bestowed on him
the name that is above every name, so that at the
name of Jesus every knee should bow, in heaven
and on earth and under the earth, and every
tongue confess that Jesus Christ is Lord, to the
glory of God the Father.[8]

The writer of Hebrews ties the example of Jesus to our own
endurance of suffering:

Looking to Jesus, the founder and perfecter of
our faith, who for the joy that was set before
him endured the cross, despising the shame, and
is seated at the right hand of the throne of God.
Consider him who endured from sinners such
hostility against himself, so that you may not grow
weary or fainthearted.[9]

THE CIRCLE OF LIFE

So is Jesus's answer to the peril of gluttony to seek perpetual suffering? Not at all. What we're getting at here is that the secret to real
enjoyment is respecting the circle of life, the cycles of nature that
are built into the world around us by our Creator. The often-quoted
poem from Ecclesiastes reminds us that "for everything there is a
season, and a time for every matter under heaven."[10] It continues,

"A time to be born, and a time to die; a time to plant, and a time to pluck up what is planted."

The problem with gluttony is it does not respect the seasons. It wants snowmen in August and surfboards in January. Because gluttony is always about more, more, more, it can't accept that there is an appropriate time for all things, and God often makes room for us to enjoy new blessings by decreasing others.

The people of God in both the Old and New Testament worlds embodied this respect for seasons in their sacred calendars. The Jewish worship was divided into daily, monthly, and yearly cycles—morning and evening sacrifices daily, weekly Sabbath worship, monthly new moon festivals, and the annual holidays such as Passover and Atonement.

Likewise, throughout most of Christian history the seasons of Lent leading up to Easter and Advent leading up to Christmas have been celebrated along with weekly worship on Sundays and daily morning and evening prayers. Contemporary churches that have moved away from such regular liturgy may have good reasons for choosing not to follow the traditional calendar, but we must acknowledge that something is lost when we ignore the seasons.

Even the secular world of retail shopping has found value in its own "liturgy" of decorating stores for various holidays and changes of season throughout the year. We can complain about how silly it is to go from Valentine's Day pink to St. Patrick's Day green, or the way they put up Christmas decorations on November 1, just after they take down the spiders and witches of Halloween. But in a sense, they are just tapping into that deep need we have to live by a calendar in tune with the seasons.

RHYTHM AND REFLECTION

Pastor Andy Stanley makes the point that often we strive in vain for a life of balance, when what we need is a life of rhythm.[11] Balance is static, implying we can get just the right mix in our lives at one point in time. The problem is, just when we get this delicate balance just right—between work and home, school and play, church and world, marriage and parenting, spending and saving, friends and family—some crisis comes along, bumps into us, and it all comes crashing down.

On the other hand, rhythm allows for an understanding that, at various times and seasons, we may need to put more focus and energy into a particular part of life. We don't have to feel guilty about giving attention to that big project at work, provided we also have a season when we can take a vacation, get away, and focus on family time. We may even find that for a season we need to give more time and attention to one child than to another as he or she passes through a particularly difficult life transition.

Of course, the key to rhythm is reflection. A good drummer has to listen to himself and the other instruments in the band to sense whether everyone is staying together. For life to stay on beat, we need to set aside time to look back and ask, "What have I been giving time, energy, and attention to? What sufferings, losses, and sorrows have I endured? What joys, gains, and delights have I celebrated?" Then we can look forward and ask, "In what people, places, and activities do I need to invest more in the next season of life? Where do I need to cut back?"

This need for reflection is one of the purposes behind the principle of Sabbath. In the law of Moses, the seventh day (Saturday) was set aside for rest, and all work was prohibited, literally on pain of death. Jesus set aside the strict Sabbath rules, especially the man-made additions to God's law that had resulted in Sabbath being used to restrict people rather than to bring them life and healing. However, the principle of Sabbath—the need for a regular day of rest and freedom from burdens—was not set aside. It predated the Ten Commandments, going all the way back to Genesis, when God created the world in six days and rested on the seventh. As people created in the image of God, we too need regular days of rest, both to restore our bodies and to reorient our lives.

Lack of Sabbath may be one of the greatest sins I see in twenty-first-century suburban parents. In God's plan, even donkeys got a day off. But we seem intent on driving our children to exhaustion. We sign them up and drive them all over town for every sport, every lesson, every extracurricular program, as if some unseen force were grading our parenting on quantity of activity rather than quality of relationship. We think we're helping, but our children don't have time to breathe, much less play. Or pray.

If your computer starts acting up and you call tech support, have you ever noticed that the first thing they ask is, "Have you rebooted your computer?" Restarting a device has amazing powers. Ninety-five percent of the time the problem seems to simply go away when you start over from the beginning.

Honoring a Sabbath is like a reboot for your soul. It lets you reset your priorities and renew your focus and energy.

Get Practical: Three Wolf Tamers

The good news is that by taming the wolf of gluttony early on, we can spare our children from its destructive influence and equip them to truly enjoy life the way God designed it. Here are three practical ways to do it.

1. Sanctify the schedule.

Today's busy families can find it hard to live by a consistent schedule, but as we've seen, timing is the key to overcoming gluttony. With all the forces at work pulling families apart, you may never find the perfect schedule, but it's important, nevertheless, to keep fighting for the schedule. If you simply give in to the chaos, gluttony is almost certain to take root.

There are two extreme parenting types: fly-by-the-seat-of-your-pants parents who may need to work diligently to force themselves to get organized, and drill-sergeant parents who may have to lighten up and be willing to bend the rules occasionally. Often in a marriage, one partner tends to be the schedule keeper and the other the schedule breaker. By making the schedule a priority and working together to determine when it's appropriate to bend the rules, you are more likely to keep your family in rhythm.

Having a set time to rise in the morning avoids the gluttony of always wanting more sleep. Equally important, though, is setting a time to go to bed—for children and for adults. That temptation to stay up just a little longer surfing the Internet, watching TV, or reading after the kids have gone to bed can be another subtle example of gluttony, because it disrespects your basic need for sleep and restoration.

Having at least one meal around the table together as a family each day has enormous benefits for creating emotional bonds and providing opportunities for meaningful conversation. A side benefit, though, is that when children have to set the table or wait for the table to be set and then wait for everyone to be served before eating, they learn to control their appetite for food in a way they can never do when they are given complete freedom to snack whenever they want.

Honoring a weekly Sabbath is important not only to teach children to make time for worship but also to break the hold of gluttony. Any area of life that demands attention seven days a week, whether it is work, school, sports, or hobbies, threatens to become a slave master over us. Remember, Sabbath is a concept, not a set of rules. For one person, running or golfing on a day off may be a great way to commune with nature and reconnect with God. For another, if golf becomes something you always want more, more, more of, setting a time limit where you say "At least once a week I'm not going to do anything related to golf," is a way to curb gluttony. In the same way, whenever you see your children becoming obsessed with a particular activity, it may be a good idea to restrict that activity on certain days of the week or even certain hours of the day. The point is to learn that everything is good in its own season, not when it's engaged in continually, without breaks.

On an annual basis, setting aside time for a family vacation is important. Even if your budget doesn't allow for expensive travel, simply taking time off and intentionally spending time together has tremendous value. However, don't think only in terms of entertainment or relaxation. Identify times of the year, whether it's in January at the start of the year, early autumn before school begins, or some other time to evaluate how things are going for each person in your home. Set goals and evaluate priorities so you stay on track spiritually, mentally, and physically.

When you are tempted to feel as though taking a break is going to put you behind, remember the example of the late S. Truett Cathy. When he started his Chick-fil-A chain of fast-food restaurants, people thought he was crazy to close on Sundays. But today they make as much in six days as many of their competitors do in seven, while their employees are doubtless much more refreshed and energized. Sabbath has a way of paying us back, and then some.

2. Teach fasting and feasting.

Fasting is the practice of abstaining for a period of time from something good, most commonly food, in order to give more time and attention to prayer. As a spiritual discipline, it has fallen into disuse among many Christians, but it is well worth reviving.

Those who practice regular fasting often report that while their physical senses are being deprived for a time, their spiritual senses become sharper. Fasting is also associated with humility and repentance. I have made regular fasting a part of my own personal spiritual disciplines for several years, and have experienced both the greater spiritual sensitivity and the nurturing of a repentant heart that it can produce.

Interestingly, fasting is never commanded by God, but Jesus does promise a reward to those who do it with the right heart attitude. He says, "And when you fast, do not look gloomy like the hypocrites, for they disfigure their faces that their fasting may be seen by others. Truly, I say to you, they have received their reward. But when you fast, anoint your head and wash your face, that your fasting may not be seen by others but by your Father who is in secret. And your Father who sees in secret will reward you."[12]

Remember, gluttony tells us happiness comes from continually getting more and more, while God's way teaches us real joy comes on the other side of seasons of suffering and loss. Intentional fasting is a way to build that process into our lives on a regular basis.

Of course, young children shouldn't be asked to go without food. And since God never forces us to fast, I would say that even teenagers should never be told they *must* fast, although they can be invited to fast with you if they so choose.

However, the principle of fasting can still be taught to our children. The practice of giving up some luxury during the season of Lent (the forty days leading up to Easter), such as sweets or sodas, can be very meaningful even for a child. Advent (the four weeks leading up to Christmas) is also a traditional season of repentance and fasting that has been largely lost in our culture. You can also declare your own seasons of fasting, during which times you might abstain from eating out or deliberately simplify the meals you prepare. Eating is such a fundamental activity of life that any change we make in our usual patterns can be a powerful way to teach symbolic lessons to our children that can make an even greater impact than the words we say.

The whole point of fasting, though, is lost if we don't place an equal emphasis on feasting. After the repentance, humility, and suffering of Lent and Advent come the great celebrations of Easter and Christmas. While God does not command fasts, He does command feasts. Repeatedly we are told in Scripture to rejoice and celebrate God's mighty acts of salvation, giving thanks for His goodness to us with food and drink, music and dancing.

In fact, Jesus was so into feasting with his friends that he was accused by the religious people of his day of being a glutton. What they did not understand was that Jesus was simply on a different schedule. He was feasting while they were fasting, but both were a part of his life. He would take up the cross and embrace its suffering willingly on Good Friday before feasting again with his disciples after the Resurrection.

In a world where our children are frequently told that following Christ takes all the fun out of life, our families need to see that we are just as intentional about saying yes to the joy of the Lord as we are about saying no to the short-lived pleasures of sin. In our family, we make a big deal out of the holidays, as well as personal celebrations such as birthdays and anniversaries. We want our children to understand that faith does not make us sour-faced killjoys. On the contrary, "everything created by God is good, and nothing is to be rejected if it is received with thanksgiving."[13]

As far back as the ancient Greeks, we have been told the secret to happiness and health is moderation—not too much and not too little. Doctors today tell us the same thing. While moderation is the path of wisdom on an everyday basis, the beauty of the spiritual life is it embraces seasons of fasting, seasons of feasting, times of simplicity, and times of celebration.

3. Don't forget the electronics.

One form of gluttony, characteristic to our time in history, is the temptation to be consumed with electronic entertainment and communication media. Over the past century, mass media such as radio and television, and now social media with its associated devices—personal computers, smartphones, and tablets—have been enormous forces for good, including opening up new frontiers to share the gospel and create connections between people who would otherwise be isolated.

However, there is also no denying the addictive nature these devices can have. Previous generations worried that too much TV would turn their kids' brains to mush. Today's generation still has that concern, along with the new concerns about video games and screen time. And it's not just the children. Getting an adult to put down the smartphone or cut the cord from email, text messaging, and social media can be just as difficult.

The form of temptation is new, but I suggest that the principles for handling it are not. Set a schedule and budget a certain amount of time when your children can be in front of the screen during the day. Observe Sabbath and make it a part of your regular weekly time of rest to unplug from media. Finally, practice fasting and feasting. Consider having seasons where you voluntarily disconnect from a particular form of media for a period of time—but also be willing to indulge in a day-long movie marathon or family video game tournament from time to time.

Remember, gluttony doesn't equate with enjoying the good things in the world; it is the temptation to obsess over more and more of a particular good thing without regard to the cycles and seasons of life.

In a chapter on the deadly sin of gluttony, you might have expected me to write more about discipline, self-control, and saying no to temptation. All of those things are important. However, I am convinced the ultimate cure for the destructive slavery to *more* is to learn how to practice the real meaning of these instructions from the Bible: "Rejoice always, pray without ceasing, give thanks in all circumstances; for this is the will of God in Christ Jesus for you."[14]

Chapter 7

THE EASY LIFE IS
THE GOOD LIFE

The Deadly Sin of Sloth

10 WAYS TO RUIN YOUR CHILD'S LIFE THROUGH SLOTH

1. Work is for fools. You're smart enough to get around it.
2. Know what's required on a job so you don't do anything extra.
3. Don't let making a life get in the way of making a living.
4. The purpose of all learning is to make money. Otherwise, why bother expanding your mind?
5. Happiness comes from eliminating risk. Don't do anything new if there's a chance of loss.
6. Teach your kids to cut their losses. If you fail at something once, don't do it any more.
7. Dreaming, not planning, is what gets things done.
8. Don't let your kids try things on their own. They might fail if you're not there to guide them every step of the way.
9. Manage your expectations. You're probably not going to be great at anything.
10. You can do it—tomorrow!

THE TWO RACES

My older daughter is a long-distance runner who has enjoyed a successful track record through high school. She has been awarded a scholarship and will continue to compete at the collegiate level. One of the things I have learned about cross-country running is every race really has two races inside of it. The first is against your competitors—to win, obviously, you have to be faster than the other runners. The second race is against yourself—and in many ways, this is the more difficult of the two. To push yourself to perform to the best of your ability, through pain and exhaustion, requires a tremendous amount of self-discipline. The rewards when you cross the finish line, however, are tremendous, and setting a new personal best can be just as rewarding as earning a medal.

The beauty of athletics is it makes that relationship between effort and reward self-evident. In many areas of life, the link is not so clear. The benefits we desire often come only after hours or months of hard work that don't feel fun at all. When it seems too difficult to reach the goal, the temptation is to simply change the goal. That's what the sixth deadly sin is all about.

In some ways, sloth, or laziness, is the inverse of lust. With lust, we must learn that saying no to a small amount of pleasure today can save us from a great deal of pain down the road. With sloth, we must learn that accepting a small amount of pain today can open the door to a great deal of pleasure down the road. Both are about developing the imagination—the faith—to visualize the future consequences of small, everyday decisions.

When I was still in high school, I got a job as a sandwich artist at the local Subway restaurant. One day the owner walked in and fired the manager. To my surprise, he then offered me the job, for the whopping salary of $1,000 a month. I thought I was rich! I will always be thankful for that experience for a couple of reasons. First, instead of resenting the boss, I learned how much harder it was to *be* the boss. I had to be up early to open the store, stay late to close it, and solve problems all day in between—at the same time I was trying to balance work with school and sports. Second, I learned $1,000 doesn't go nearly as far as I had thought. Most important, though, I'm thankful for that early work experience because it taught me the satisfaction inherent in a good day's work well done.

LESSONS FROM THE ANTHILL

The classic biblical warning against sloth is found in the book of Proverbs:

> Go to the ant, O sluggard;
>   consider her ways, and be wise.
> Without having any chief,
>   officer, or ruler,
> she prepares her bread in summer
>   and gathers her food in harvest.

> How long will you lie there, O sluggard?
>   When will you arise from your sleep?
> A little sleep, a little slumber,
>   a little folding of the hands to rest,
> and poverty will come upon you like a robber,
>   and want like an armed man.[1]

Ants are amazing creatures. Just watching them, it's easy to be impressed with how industrious they are, constantly working to build their homes and gather food. As the text points out, they are aware of the importance of seasons. They gather more food than they need during the summer months when food is plentiful so they have a store left over to subsist on during the winter months. In contrast, the sluggard, or habitually lazy person, doesn't do the work today because he does not anticipate the coming of future needs. Poverty jumps him like a street thug in a dark alley.

However, most interesting about this description is what the writer of Proverbs points out about the ant's motivation: It has no "chief, officer, or ruler." No one bosses the ant around. Sure, there is a queen ant, but she just lays eggs. She doesn't tell the ants what to do; they do it all on their own. They have an instinct that functions as an internal boss. The lazy man doesn't have that. Given the option to get up and work or push the snooze button, he chooses just a few more minutes of sleep—and a few more, and a few more, until the opportunities of life are wasted.

Sloth is not always evident when there is an external boss. The person who gets up on time for school or work, does assignments on time, and even sweats out the grunt work may still be lazy at heart.

It all depends on the motivation. You may work really hard when it's required of you, but do you require it of yourself? Do your children do the work only when they have to—when someone is watching over them, telling them what to do—or, like the ant, can they function on their own without a supervisor? Have they developed that internal boss?

One way to measure sloth is what you or your children do with free time. There is a time for rest and relaxation—remember the discussion of Sabbath in the previous chapter. However, when you are well rested and find yourself with a few minutes on your hands, do you ever choose to do anything creative? Do you read a book, watch something educational, create something with your imagination, dream up an idea to make the world a better place? Or do you burn the time watching pointless TV or playing the latest Angry Birds app? Both the lazy person and the diligent person work hard when they have to; the difference is that given the choice, the lazy person takes the easy way out, while the diligent person has the internal motivation to accomplish something worthwhile.

SLEEP IS NOT YOUR ENEMY

We should pause here to note that sleep is not the same thing as sloth. God created sleep, and He calls it a good gift: "It is in vain that you rise up early and go late to rest, eating the bread of anxious toil; for he gives to his beloved sleep."[2]

As we saw in the chapter on greed, the principle of Sabbath rest is one of God's commands that we ignore at our peril. Too many people today are ruining their health because fear and worry rob them of their ability to sleep in peace. Other people don't get the rest they need because they are perfectionists. They put expectations on themselves that they must do everything, be everything, and look great doing it. They take pride in being martyrs, suffering with heavy burdens, but those burdens don't come from God. Remember, Jesus said, "My yoke is easy, and my burden is light."[3] We certainly don't want to pass that on to our children by teaching them, directly or indirectly, that you have to be exhausted all the time to be a good person.

In fact, if you are fatigued all the time, or if one of your children is, it would be good to visit a doctor. Many medical problems can cause undue tiredness. For example, my coauthor, Ken, suffers from sleep apnea. For several years he kept pushing himself, thinking he was being lazy when he would become drowsy in the middle of the day. Only after his wife persuaded him to see a sleep specialist did he realize he wasn't breathing well at night. For Ken, the promise "God gives to his beloved sleep" came about through a machine that helps keep his airway open. The deadly sin of sloth is a matter of the heart, not one of the many physical conditions that wear down our bodies.

If sleep is not the problem, neither is busyness the goal. Have you noticed that if you ask someone how he or she is doing, the number one answer is fine, but the second answer, if you press a little harder, is busy. We are a nation that takes great pride in staying busy. We complain about how much we have to do, but our complaining is really a form of bragging. We don't consider ourselves successful as parents unless we have our children playing on two sports teams and learning to play a musical instrument and speaking a foreign language while taking drawing lessons, on top of a full schedule of homework, play dates, and church activities. And that's not even starting on our own work and volunteer schedules.

DAYDREAMS AND LIFE DREAMS

So does our national preoccupation with busyness mean we don't have a problem with sloth? Well, let me ask you this. Have you ever had a big project due at work, but you weren't sure you could do it, so you stayed busy doing a bunch of less important projects? You alphabetize your files, sort your paper clips by size, check your email fifteen times a day, update your social media profile, anything to avoid the real task that needs to be done. In the 1960s Charles Hummel coined the phrase "the tyranny of the urgent"[4] to describe how we allow things such as telephone calls to control our day (today we might add email and text messages). Stephen Covey expanded on Hummel's idea to point out that often we choose to do what is urgent in place of what is important.[5]

Beyond the principles of good time management at work or school or home, however, is the bigger issue of your life calling. At some point in your journey, you have probably had a dream. An audacious idea. A vision to do something more. A stirring in your soul to confront a particular evil in the world or meet a need.

Maybe it was clear-cut for you, as it was for my wife when she was gripped by a calling for us to become foster parents and make a difference for children with no stable home. Maybe it was more cloudy, just a vague, nagging sense you should do more with your talents, such as picking up that paintbrush you haven't used since your high school art class. Maybe it seemed really spiritual, like a call to go to the mission field. Or maybe you had no idea it was from God, like a dream to start your own restaurant or write a mystery novel. Whatever it was, though, it gripped your soul deep down inside with desire—but at the same time came fear. Fear that you couldn't do it, that you could fail, that you lacked the talent or knowledge or ability. And along the way, it just seemed easier to put it off for another day, staying busy with all the activities of everyday life, than to take the risk of going down that road.

In fact, if we look back at the book of Proverbs, we find that the slothful person doesn't suffer from a lack of desire. It's not that she doesn't want to do great things. It's just that she never takes the steps of action to get started on them.

> The soul of the sluggard craves and gets nothing,
> while the soul of the diligent is richly
> supplied.

> The desire of the sluggard kills him,
> for his hands refuse to labor.

Closely related to the lazy person's lack of action is his ability to rationalize and make excuses.

> The way of a sluggard is like a hedge of thorns,
> but the path of the upright is a level highway.

The sluggard says, "There is a lion outside!
    I shall be killed in the streets!"[6]

The thorns are the obstacles and barriers that explain why the slothful person can't act today—little Johnny has a cold or things are really busy at work right now or the stock market is down or the car is broken. The lions are all the logical reasons why it would be dangerous or risky to follow the dream. When the house is paid off or the kids are out of school, maybe then he will follow the dream, but not right now.

This ability to make excuses explains why a slothful person never believes he is lazy. In his mind, he's just working smarter instead of harder, no matter how many people tell him otherwise:

The sluggard is wiser in his own eyes
    than seven men who can answer sensibly.[7]

At the end of the day, though, when all of the excuses have passed and all the rationalizations have run their course, the lazy person sits down to pursue the dream and finds the opportunity has passed—time has run out. He or she has substituted a life-time of daydreams for accomplishing the true life dream God had planned.

The movie *Spider-Man* made popular the phrase "with great power comes great responsibility." Plain, ordinary Peter Parker is given the gift of superhuman strength and abilities, but with it comes a duty to use that power for the good of humankind. Of course, that's not just true for imaginary superheroes. It's true for all of us.

You see, it's not just children with no visibly great talents or abilities who are tempted to waste their lives. On the contrary, it is precisely those who have the greatest potential who are the most tempted to throw it away. Think about it: If you were Satan, wouldn't your first target be those with extraordinary power for good? Your first plan would be to get them to use that power for evil, but failing that, the next best thing would be to get them to simply sleep their life away, wasting their days and hours on frivolous things with no lasting value.

And here's the lesson: every child is extraordinary in some way. Every son and every daughter is given the gift of God's power in some area of their lives. It's simply a matter of discovering what that calling is.

In 2 Kings 13:14–25, scripture contains a fascinating story about King Joash of Israel. In the time of Joash, God's people had been harassed and defeated for years by the Syrians to the north. Just before his death, the great prophet Elisha summoned Joash and instructed him to shoot arrows out of the window. Each arrow symbolized a victory over Syria. Joash obeyed, but he stopped after only three arrows. Elisha became angry with him. "You should have struck five or six times; then you would have struck down Syria until you had made an end of it," Elisha said, "but now you will strike down Syria only three times."[8]

When it comes to talent and ability in any given aspect of life, some people have only three arrows to shoot, while others have five or six. Someone can appear to be successful from a human point of view, but from God's viewpoint, he or she may actually be lazy. What matters is not how many victories we achieve but whether we live up to our potential. As Jesus said, "Everyone to whom much was given, of him much will be required."[9]

LAZINESS AND DISAPPOINTMENT

I find it interesting that, historically, the deadly sin of sloth was known by the name *acedia*, which means "boredom or apathy," a general sense of being weary of the world. In other words, an attitude of laziness may be an indicator that you have lost your hope.

Do you remember Aesop's fable of The Fox and the Grapes? A fox stumbles upon a tasty-looking cluster of grapes, but they are just out of his reach. After jumping several times and failing to reach them, the fox walks away, muttering to himself, "They were probably sour anyway." Like that fox, sometimes a child may become lazy and apathetic about an activity. She may claim she finds it boring or uninteresting, but in truth, it could be that she has given up hope after her initial efforts fell short.

When we give up on our faith in God's calling and purpose for our lives, we lose the motivation to act. We don't believe we are capable of greatness, so we fear trying. At that point there's little difference between those who sleep their days away, accomplishing nothing, and those who fill their days with busyness, buzzing from one activity to another and appearing to have all sorts of energy but, in actuality, going nowhere. It's the class clown who could have been the class president but, because of the risk involved in sharing a sincere belief instead of a sarcastic comment, found it easier to make others laugh than to motivate people. It's the 4.0 math major who could have been a great artist but, because someone laughed at her first painting, now prefers an ordered and predictable subject in which she can always know the right answers. It's the dropout who put no effort into school, even though he's brilliant, because he couldn't handle the pain of rejection when someone called him a nerd.

When a painful experience causes my child to numb himself with sloth, it's not enough for me to simply tell him to stop being lazy. I must help him remember his purpose and renew his hope. Purpose comes from knowing that God has a plan for my life that is worth working hard to achieve. Hope comes from knowing that God is always with me in the journey and will fulfill His promise in the end, even though I may suffer disappointments along the way. The key is having the right kind of conversation with myself and then joyfully trying to motivate my child.

Psalm 42 provides an example of such self-talk. The psalmist is seeking encouragement during a time of sadness in which he feels disappointed and distant from God:

> My tears have been my food
>   day and night,
> while they say to me all the day long,
>   "Where is your God?"
> These things I remember,
>   as I pour out my soul:
> how I would go with the throng
>   and lead them in procession to the house of God

with glad shouts and songs of praise,
    a multitude keeping festival.

Why are you cast down, O my soul,
    and why are you in turmoil within me?
Hope in God; for I shall again praise him,
    my salvation and my God.

My soul is cast down within me;
    therefore I remember you.[10]

Notice the psalmist first directs his own attention to the past: "Remember what God has done," he tells himself. "Remember the good times, when I was full of joy." Parents can help their children reconnect with God's purpose by remembering past successes and victories. We can remind ourselves and our children that, before disappointment came along, God had a plan in place.

After reflecting on the past, the psalmist shifts his focus to the future:

I say to God, my rock:
    "Why have you forgotten me?
Why do I go mourning
    because of the oppression of the enemy?"
As with a deadly wound in my bones,
    my adversaries taunt me,
while they say to me all the day long,
    "Where is your God?"

> Why are you cast down, O my soul,
>
>> and why are you in turmoil within me?
>
> Hope in God; for I shall again praise him,
>
>> my salvation and my God.[11]

Here the psalmist is telling himself, "Life won't always be this bad, things will get better, there is hope." Importantly, this hope is not just wishful thinking; it is a hope that is grounded in God. We probably shouldn't say to our children, "Work hard and all your dreams will become reality," because we don't know whether their dreams will come to fruition. We can have much more confidence if we say, "Keep working toward God's plan, and hope in God, for God never fails." Those whose hope is only in their own efforts will give up when those efforts fall short. Those whose hope is in God keep working even after they fall short, because they know that God is also working and He is faithful to complete the work He has begun. As the apostle Paul wrote, "Be steadfast, immovable, always abounding in the work of the Lord, knowing that in the Lord your labor is not in vain."[12]

My son Patrick Wilson recently taught me a lesson about not giving up. He had expressed an interest in tennis, so I lined up an instructor for him, and he worked hard for several months to learn the game. When it came time for his first real match, his coach and I agreed that he should be challenged. So, we chose to have him play up against an opponent in the twelve-and-under age division instead of the ten-and-under age division. The match was beyond challenging—his opponent destroyed him with ease in straight sets. Patrick hardly scored a point. Afterward, he was crying, and I was doubting my parental wisdom. *I've devastated his motivation,* I thought. *He'll never want to play again.*

Shortly after we came home, though, Patrick Wilson emerged from his room and asked me to go hit tennis balls with him. I was relieved—his desire to play had not been crushed. In fact, after three hours of hitting, he was still going strong. The weather was becoming uncomfortable. "It's cold and windy. Let's go home," I said. I'll never forget the deadpan look on his face when he responded, "Dad, don't you think I'll ever have to play a match when it's cold and windy?"

When we finally called it a night, I was tired and cold, but proud of my son for his resilience in the face of adversity. I only hope that I can show the same determination when I experience defeat or disappointment. I know I will if I remind myself of my purpose and renew my hope in God.

Get Practical: Three Cups of Coffee

So how do we help our children identify their strengths, push toward new personal bests, and develop an internal boss so they will be self-motivated to accomplish their life dreams? Here are three suggestions—think of them as three cups of coffee—to wake them up from a life of sloth and get them moving toward passion and purpose.

1. Upsize from the American dream.

Without a purpose in life bigger than myself, there's no real point in *not* being lazy, and the typical American dream is no longer enough.

If all we have to offer our children is "work hard in school so you can go to a good college so you can get a good job so you can make lots of money so you can retire early and take it easy," we shouldn't be surprised if they simply skip straight to the end and take it easy now.

Instead, connect them to the bigger dream of God to make disciples of Jesus Christ for the transformation of the world. Scripture tells us that God is working to put the entire cosmos right, through the saving work of Jesus, and that we are called to be a part of that process as the body of Jesus—acting as His hands and feet and voice in the world today.

Purpose comes from being a part of a story. Fill your child's world with stories of people who helped change the world. Find biographies of great men and women of faith and purpose for them to read or watch. Talk about moments in history and in your own experience together. Share with them your own stories of God's calling and purpose in your life.

Most important, tell and retell the story of God's mighty works in history given to us in Scripture. They need to hear repeatedly that God created a big, beautiful, wonderful world where He could dwell together with us, but we destroyed it through sin and brought sickness, sadness, evil, and death into it. But God did not give up on His world. Our Creator had a plan to rescue it and put everything right again—a plan that found its ultimate fulfillment through Jesus Christ's death, burial, and resurrection. God founded the church and poured out the Holy Spirit to carry on the plan to make all things right in the world in Jesus's name.

When children hear this big story—especially the last part where they can see that the story is continuing through them—they find an identity, a vision, and a purpose much bigger than any other that could be offered to them.

2. Learn how to sweeten the bitterness of defeat.

A person who has fallen into the trap of sloth is often one who has attempted great things, failed, and drawn the conclusion that it is better not to try at all. Psychologists call this learned helplessness. Parents can make this worse if they set unreasonably high expectations or express disappointment in a way that makes their children feel that their failure is permanent. This is part of why the apostle Paul warns parents (especially fathers), "Do not exasperate your children, so that they will not lose heart."[13]

Exasperating our children can often happen without our realizing it. For example, if you are good at math, your daughter may assume you expect her to be as well, even if you never say so. When she falls short of your example, she may feel like a failure. Or perhaps you had high hopes your son would be a top athlete, and when he doesn't perform well you may subconsciously communicate disappointment through your facial expressions, tone of voice, or comments. If someone asks, you would say it doesn't matter to you, but your child can sense that it does.

The only way to find out for sure if your children are experiencing discouragement is to ask them questions such as, "What are some things you think you are good at? What are some things you think you are not good at?" Then find out why they think they are not good at certain things.

Or you might ask, "Has there ever been a time when I let you down?" and listen carefully to their answers, then lead into, "Has there ever been a time when you feel as if you let me down?" The answer to both questions may surprise you.

It's also a good practice to ask them on a daily or weekly basis to share their highs and lows—things that went well for them and things that didn't go well for them that day, so you can keep your pulse on what has them excited and what might be getting them down.

This is not to say we shouldn't be realistic about failure. Part of dealing with defeat is acknowledging it is real and painful. However, we can communicate that failure does not have to be the final chapter. Everyone who has accomplished something great has failed at some point, and often the greatest life lessons are learned during adversity. As the psalmist wrote, "My flesh and my heart may fail, but God is the strength of my heart and my portion forever."[14]

The key is to recognize when failure—however your child perceives it—has led into discouragement or despair so you can find ways to uplift his or her heart. God can turn our failures into something good through His redemptive power.

3. Stir up steps of action.

The flip side of making sure your children are not discouraged by failure is to make sure you show them how to succeed—in clear, practical terms. Often we think we are teaching our children to succeed when what we are really doing is just putting more pressure on them.

Consider a child who is having trouble with physics. You can say, "Keep trying! You can do it! I believe in you!" all you want to, but if the child doesn't understand the steps involved in solving the problem, he or she isn't going to be able to do it and will eventually conclude that all your cheerleading is worthless.

What's true for school is equally true in the bigger issues of your life dream. Many people have dreams of doing great things, but they don't know how to get them done. They haven't learned the discipline of stating the current reality and the preferred future, identifying the critical factors necessary to get from point A to point B, and breaking those critical factors down into small, tangible steps of action.

Do you feel called to write a novel? You need to make an outline. Form your characters. Determine your setting. Take a writing class. Find a good editor. And most important, start writing a little every day, whether of good or bad quality. Novels don't write themselves. Whatever the big goal, break it down into smaller, achievable sub-goals.

As parents, we tend to go to the extremes of either letting our kids do whatever they want or giving them precise instructions on how to do a job so they don't have to think for themselves. Instead, sometimes we need to give our children projects. Paint a room. Build a tree house. Buy a used car. Whatever it is, set the parameters to stay within (as with a budget) and clarify the criteria for success. Talk them through forming their own plan to accomplish it. Then—and this is the hard part—walk away and let them implement their plan. After they are done, come back and evaluate the results with them and help them identify lessons on how to improve their plan next time.

It's hard not to micromanage our children because we don't want to see them fail (and it can be just as hard on our pride if they succeed but don't do it the way we would have done it). However, the life lessons learned outweigh the costs because they gain the confidence that when God gives them a life dream, they can take action on it instead of just daydreaming for the rest of their lives.

As we've seen, the best step you can take to ensure your children don't fall into the trap of a deadly sin is to assess whether you yourself are giving in to its temptation.

Are you fulfilling your God-given potential? Have you substituted a lesser dream for the life dream He has called you to, one that is part of His bigger purpose and plan in history? Are you taking measurable steps of action toward that dream? And when you fall down, are you getting back up again? If fear and discouragement are holding you down, take heart. Hear the word of the Lord: "Have I not commanded you? Be strong and courageous. Do not be frightened, and do not be dismayed, for the LORD your God is with you wherever you go."[15]

Giving in to sloth can ruin your child's life. Having the courage to pursue your calling is the key that can unlock not only your own fulfillment but also the joy of seeing your children discover and fulfill their own potential in Christ.

Chapter 8

IF YOU DON'T GET YOUR WAY, GET MAD!

The Deadly Sin of Wrath

10 WAYS TO RUIN YOUR CHILD'S LIFE THROUGH ANGER

1. Rights are for you. Responsibilities are for other people.
2. Ignore the injustices in the world; they might distract you from your own problems.
3. Let your kids hear you curse and yell when someone irritates you, so they'll know how important it is to stand up for themselves.
4. When it comes to discipline, go with the flow. Whatever you feel in the heat of the moment is probably right.
5. Change the rules frequently.
6. Never apologize. The past is the past. *Hakuna matata.*
7. When kids fight, the main thing is for them to not bother you. They'll figure it out.
8. Model morality by pointing out everyone else's sins.
9. Teach your children that, as Christians, we are morally superior to all other people.
10. Model for your children the main point of the whole Bible: God's mad at you.

THE GIFT OF ANGER

I will never forget my fourth trip to Haiti. The church I serve sent a team to explore the next steps in our involvement with that nation. My first visit had been three years before, not long after the devastating earthquake of 2010 that leveled huge parts of the capital city, Port-au-Prince, and left tens of thousands homeless. There we found a community of deaf individuals who had gathered in one of the many makeshift tent cities that sprang up. During the years that followed, we had the tremendous privilege of partnering with leaders from the deaf community and two Christian missions organizations to provide housing, a church, and a school for 168 deaf families, along with clean water, educational sponsorships, and opportunities for job training. It was quite a journey, full of rewarding stories of the power of Christ to transform lives.

But it was on my fourth trip that I learned a new word: *restavek*. It means "to stay with" and refers to children sent to live with families as household slaves. It is estimated that three hundred thousand children in this tiny, impoverished island nation, some as young as my own preschool daughter, are kept in bondage and forced to do menial labor.

I had been somewhat aware of the modern slavery issue and had heard leaders such as Gary Haugen of International Justice Mission explain that, globally, there are more people in slavery today—an estimated twenty-seven million—than in the entire history of the African slave trade. Many of those are women and girls, abducted and placed into brothels by the horrific sex trafficking industry. Through another mission agency our church supports, I had even met orphaned girls from the Eastern European nation of Moldova who had been rescued from situations where they were at high risk of becoming slaves.

What made this trip to Haiti different was that I actually met a child whom I later learned might have been a restavek. Unbeknownst to me at the time, I was actually seeing and talking to a little one in need of rescue.

In a word, I was furious. I wanted to fly back down to Haiti, find that child, and take him home with me. I wanted to punish the people who had used him like an animal instead of loving him as a human being. I wanted to single-handedly take on the entire Haitian government for allowing this to go on day after day, turning a blind eye to the evil right under their noses. I wanted justice.

I begin this chapter on anger with this story because I want to establish one thing right off the bat: anger is a gift from God. We are supposed to get angry. God gets angry. He says so over and over in Scripture (and not just in the Old Testament, for those who think Jesus's coming somehow changed God's character). The thing about God is, He doesn't get angry just because He doesn't get His way (ultimately, He always gets His way). God gets angry because of injustice. He gets angry because the strong, the powerful, the privileged, and those who are supposed to know better *abuse* and *oppress* the weak, the poor, and the powerless. And He expects us to get angry about that too—angry enough to take action.

What makes anger a deadly sin is when we take the gift God gave us to fight injustice and instead use it as a weapon to get our own way. Sinful anger is the opposite of Jesus's prayer in the garden of Gethsemane. In effect the wrathful person says, "Not Thy will, but mine be done, and I'll crucify anyone who gets in my way!" Sinful anger is putting myself on the throne of the universe, declaring myself to be god and king and bringing down wrath on any who dare to defy me. It would almost be laughable, if its effects on people weren't so devastating.

IN HIS IMAGE

Like pride and lust and all of the other deadly sins we have covered, the great tragedy of sinful anger is that it defaces and deforms who we were fundamentally created to be. We are told in Genesis that we were created in the image of God. We read, "Then God said, 'Let us make man in our image, after our likeness. And let them have dominion over the fish of the sea and over the birds of the heavens and over the livestock and over all the earth and over every creeping thing that creeps on the earth.'"[1]

We were made to be the living images representing God's rule to all of creation, and as vice rulers on God's behalf, we are given power and authority over creation in order to maintain justice.

Sin has corrupted the image of God within us, but our core mission to rule on God's behalf has not been rescinded. David wrote in one of his songs:

> When I consider Your heavens,
> the work of Your fingers,
> The moon and the stars,
> which You have ordained;
> What is man that You take thought of him,
> And the son of man that You care for him?
> Yet You have made him a little lower than God,
> And You crown him with glory and majesty!
> You make him to rule over the works of Your
> hands;
> You have put all things under his feet.[2]

How important to God is this human role of ruling with justice? Scripture says in Proverbs that it is more important than even worship: "To do righteousness and justice is desired by the LORD more than sacrifice."[3]

The prophet Micah summarizes the whole duty of humankind this way: "He has told you, O man, what is good; and what does the LORD require of you but to do justice, and to love kindness, and to walk humbly with your God?"[4]

In case we miss the point, Isaiah makes it extremely plain how strongly God feels:

"What are your multiplied sacrifices to Me?" Says
the LORD.
"I have had enough of burnt offerings of rams
And the fat of fed cattle;
And I take no pleasure in the blood of bulls,
lambs or goats ...
"Bring your worthless offerings no longer,
Incense is an abomination to Me.
New moon and sabbath, the calling of assem-
blies—I cannot endure iniquity and the solemn
assembly. "I hate your new moon festivals and
your appointed feasts,
They have become a burden to Me;
I am weary of bearing them.
"So when you spread out your hands in prayer,
I will hide My eyes from you;
Yes, even though you multiply prayers,
I will not listen.
Your hands are covered with blood.
"Wash yourselves, make yourselves clean;
Remove the evil of your deeds from My sight.
Cease to do evil,
Learn to do good; Seek justice,
Reprove the ruthless,
Defend the orphan,
Plead for the widow."[5]

Clearly, justice is kind of a big deal to God.

RIGHTS AND RIGHTEOUSNESS

When you consider the scope of humanity's calling to create justice and compare it to the vast evils in the world today—millions in slavery, people who starve to death every day because of corrupt governments, women and children abused, refugees driven from their homes by senseless wars—the things we actually get angry about on a daily basis become utterly ridiculous.

Just think about the last time you drove your car. Have you ever yelled at someone for cutting you off in traffic? fumed about the guy riding too close to your bumper? grumbled because someone swept into the parking space you were waiting for? Be honest; I don't think I'm the only one who does those things. But then I think, *Really, Patrick? There are children in slavery right now in Haiti and around the world, and you are going to get angry about a piece of pavement you thought you had a right to?*

That is the heart of sinful anger: confusing my rights with God's righteousness. It's not our sense of fairness that is to blame nor our belief that there is a right and a wrong way for the world to be ordered—the right way involving respect, dignity, and equal treatment. The problem is, we twist that sense to only be concerned about ourselves and what is right for us, while ignoring what is right for others. We want to be treated fairly, even as we treat others unfairly.

Consider these examples of the relationship between anger and rights:

I get angry when ...	Because I have a right to ...	Yet I ...
someone interrupts me while I am talking.	have my thoughts and opinions heard.	routinely interrupt others when I suddenly have a great idea to share.
someone keeps me waiting.	schedule my own time.	routinely show up late because I was busy doing something important.
someone gossips about me.	have my reputation respected.	routinely gossip about others behind their backs.

We could go on listing examples, but the apostle Paul summarizes it for us: "Therefore you have no excuse, O man, every one of you who judges. For in passing judgment on another you condemn yourself, because you, the judge, practice the very same things."[6]

In other words, we're all hypocrites. We're all guilty of doing the very same things we get angry at others for doing.

Jesus asked, "Can a blind man lead a blind man? Will they not both fall into a pit?"[7] Imagine an eye surgeon offering to do LASIK surgery on you, while at the same time bumping into walls because his glasses are so dirty he can't see where he's going. That's what God sees every time we get angry and judgmental about the sins of others while completely ignoring, excusing, or justifying our own wicked hearts.

EVERY CHILD A LAWYER

Children have an extremely refined sense of justice. I'm pretty sure if I gave one of my children a hundred jelly beans and another ninety-nine, the cheated one would instantly notice the difference and raise a protest. No sooner are they able to speak than our children become little lawyers, arguing their cases for why they aren't being treated fairly. I'm sure I'm not the only one who has observed a child getting bumped into or shoved by accident, then looking around to see if Mom or Dad is present before deciding if he or she is hurt enough to cry. Sometimes kids almost seem to relish the experience of getting hurt if it means an opportunity to get someone else in trouble.

How should a parent respond when faced with this barrage of constant bickering? One easy way out is to choose peace at any cost. We make statements such as, "I don't care who started it, just be quiet and stop arguing." Of course, in our hearts we know that's not a solution. Being quiet isn't teaching children how to overcome anger; it's just teaching them to be subtle enough to keep it hushed.

If you have read this far, you are an engaged parent, so I doubt you give in very often to the "just be quiet" method. More common is the second mistake that I call "jumping to Jesus."

It may surprise you that a Christian pastor would say this, but sometimes I think we are too quick to apply the teachings of Jesus to our children. Let me explain. Loving your enemies, turning the other cheek, and forgiveness are at the heart of Jesus's teachings. Certainly we want to teach those messages to our children, both in word and in deed. After all, our ultimate goal as parents is to participate with the Holy Spirit in forming our children to be like Jesus, the one who prayed, "Father, forgive them," from the cross.

However, think for a moment about how God our heavenly Father parented his children, the people of Israel. God gave them the Torah, the law of Moses, hundreds of years before he gave them Jesus teachings. The Law says little about forgiveness, but a great deal about justice.[8] The apostle Paul explains that Torah is "our tutor to lead us to Christ."[9] By first establishing an absolute standard of right and wrong, God prepared His people to receive His forgiveness, mercy, and grace through faith in Jesus.

You see, forgiveness and mercy only make sense within the context of justice. If there is no law broken, what is there to be forgiven? If there is no punishment for sin, who needs mercy? If there's no such thing as sin, what was the point of Jesus dying on the cross?

We need to see that the law is right and good and that we have broken the law and sinned before God before we are ready to receive salvation. In the same way, children need to experience an environment where set rules and standards of behavior, along with clear consequences, are applied consistently and without favoritism before they can understand what it means to forgive. In other words, they need law before grace.

Here's my experience: in an environment of justice where the rules are fair and consistent, children are actually better than adults at practicing forgiveness. However, in an unfair environment, "forgiveness" can become just one more weapon in the arsenal of the bullies. They hurt others and then demand to be forgiven. They learn to glibly say "I'm sorry" without anything resembling true repentance, like a magic spell that renders them impervious to retaliation.

Again, that's not to say we should be content with producing little legalists. Ultimately we must make it our goal to teach them the mercy and grace of Christ who says to forgive "not seven times, but seventy times seven times." However, the best way to teach that is, once again, through our own example. When they see us practice forgiveness toward those who hurt us, and when they experience mercy for their own faults and failures, they will have a better foundation for extending mercy to others than if we simply order them to forgive one another without addressing their sense of fairness and justice.

Get Practical: Three Temper Tamers

So how do we go about conquering anger in ourselves and in our children? Here are three practical steps.

1. Respect the power of language.

As parents, we sometimes tend to prioritize physical acts over verbal ones when correcting our children. The child who hits or bites or scratches naturally seems like a greater problem than the one who uses insulting words. However, Jesus ties the two together:

> You have heard that it was said to those of old, "You
> shall not murder; and whoever murders will be

liable to judgment." But I say to you that everyone who is angry with his brother will be liable to judgment; whoever insults his brother will be liable to the council; and whoever says, "You fool!" will be liable to the hell of fire.[10]

James, another writer in the New Testament, also reminds us of the enormous power of the tongue in strong terms:

So also the tongue is a small member, yet it boasts of great things. How great a forest is set ablaze by such a small fire! And the tongue is a fire, a world of unrighteousness. The tongue is set among our members, staining the whole body, setting on fire the entire course of life, and set on fire by hell. For every kind of beast and bird, of reptile and sea creature, can be tamed and has been tamed by mankind, but no human being can tame the tongue. It is a restless evil, full of deadly poison. With it we bless our Lord and Father, and with it we curse people who are made in the likeness of God. From the same mouth come blessing and cursing. My brothers, these things ought not to be so.[11]

Therefore, the starting point for dealing with anger is our words. First of all, make it a point to never speak with disrespect toward your spouse. When a husband belittles, puts down, and insults his wife, he undercuts her authority with her children and teaches them to use words to harm others rather than to protect and nurture them. Likewise, a wife who speaks ill of her husband, whether to his face or behind his back, sows seeds of bitterness in the family as the children implicitly feel pulled to choose sides and take up offenses. Bottom line, you'll never make any progress with anger in your children if the adults can't show respect for one another.

Second, cut out cursing. Sometimes Christians have made a bigger deal out of foul language than is probably warranted. The occasional swear word when you hit your thumb with a hammer is not nearly as bad as a life dominated by gluttony or envy. However, cursing directed by parents toward children or by children toward parents and others in anger reflects deep-seated rage. It is horribly dehumanizing to label another person with a curse, and what we use to dehumanize others also ends up dehumanizing us. We ought to take verbal abuse just as seriously as physical abuse for the protection of the abused and the salvation of the abuser.

Finally, teach children how to express feelings rather than fling labels. One way to do this is to show them how to make *I* statements instead of *you* statements. For example, instead of "You are such a thief, you always take my clothes," a child could say, "I feel like you don't respect my property when you borrow my clothes without asking." *You* statements are accusatory and evoke a defensive retaliation, whereas *I* statements are vulnerable and invite a disarmed response. Labels such as *thief, liar,* and *pest* attack the person, leaving no option but to fight back, whereas objective descriptions such as "when you take my clothes" or "when you promise me you'll do something and then change your mind" separate the behavior from the person and leave room for discussion.

2. Work out discipline ahead of time.

Perhaps the easiest place for a parent to fall into anger is in the discipline process. Teaching and instruction will only go so far. Eventually every child needs more than words to correct wrong behavior. However, in imposing consequences, we don't want to give way to unbridled anger or rage. One key to keeping ourselves under control is to work out a plan ahead of time.

Together with your spouse, identify your children's most common behavior issues and write rules for your family. Then determine what consequences follow if the rules are violated. If your children are old enough to have a conversation about the topic, you might invite them to share what an appropriate consequence would be for a violation. Write these rules and consequences on a chart and post it on the refrigerator or some other conspicuous place in your house. That way, the guidelines are worked out while you are calm and level headed, not in the heat of the moment. Children will better understand that the punishment is the logical consequence of breaking the rule, not an arbitrary decision you made on a whim, and you will be less tempted to over- or undercorrect them based on your mood at the time.

Of course, situations will come up that aren't on the chart, and extenuating circumstances will arise that dictate a deviation from the plan. However, you'll be able to do this with greater wisdom and justice if you work from an established plan than if you are completely making it up from scratch as you go along.

3. Keep short accounts.

When anger does flare up, deal with it in a timely manner. The apostle Paul gives the basic rule of thumb in his letter to the Ephesians: "Be angry and do not sin; do not let the sun go down on your anger, and give no opportunity to the devil."[12] Anger that is left to simmer overnight has a way of growing into deep-rooted bitterness that is much more difficult to weed out.

One way to ensure the sundown statute is to make releasing anger a part of your evening prayer routine. When you put your children to bed, prayers of thanksgiving for the day are wonderful, as are prayers asking for God's blessings on those whom we love. However, if we are to pray as Jesus taught us to pray, we need to also include confession of sin ("forgive us our debts"), which necessarily includes releasing anger ("as we also have forgiven our debtors")— since "if you forgive others their trespasses, your heavenly Father will also forgive you, but if you do not forgive others their trespasses, neither will your Father forgive your trespasses."[13]

What if you (or your children) don't feel like forgiving? The trick is not to think harder about having loving feelings toward those who have hurt us but to think more about your own need for forgiveness from God. Scripture never gives a formula for how to forgive others. Instead, over and over we are told, forgive "as God in Christ forgave you."[14]

We have a tendency to revisit the pain others inflicted on us, visualizing it again and again in our minds, when we should instead revisit the cross. Visualize Jesus hanging there and ask yourself, "Did I need this? Did Jesus waste His blood? Am I such a good person that I did not need Him to give His life for my forgiveness? If not—if I am a sinner in need of God's mercy at the cost of His very Son's life—then who am I to withhold forgiveness from others?"

If we do hold on to anger past sundown, we certainly should not hold on to it past the taking of Communion. However often your church practices the sacrament of the Lord's Supper, don't allow yourself to partake of the body and blood of Christ without examining yourself first to see if there is any offense you need to let go of. It is impossible to truly understand the meaning of the Lord's Table and yet hold on to anger, bitterness, and unforgiveness.

Anger is a terrible fire that can consume a family and leave disfiguring scars for years to come. On the other hand, a family that learns to overcome anger can enjoy an unbelievable amount of peace—and make a difference in the world for justice.

Chapter 9

BECOMING WHO YOU ARE

The Seven Cardinal Virtues

10 WAYS TO RUIN YOUR CHILD'S LIFE THROUGH DISTORTING THE VIRTUES

1. Virtue means being a naive goody-goody with no concept of the real world.
2. Humility means putting yourself down.
3. Chastity means being a prude and never enjoying anything.
4. Kindness means acting nice to people you don't really like.
5. Charity means giving just enough money away in public that people think you are a good person—plus it's a tax deduction.
6. Temperance means having enough willpower to "just say no" without help from anyone.
7. Diligence means feeling as if you've never worked hard enough or long enough.
8. Patience means suffering in silence because it won't do any good to complain.
9. Vice is always more fun than virtue, but God doesn't like fun.
10. Virtue means conforming. Your vices make you unique.

THE OTHER SEVEN

Now that we have explored all seven of the deadly sins than can ruin a child, it's time to turn our attention to the seven cardinal virtues—the positive traits God desires for us to nurture in our children in place of those sins.

Recently while preparing for a sermon, I discovered a musical term I was not familiar with: *tessitura*. It refers to the strength range for a voice—not necessarily the highest or lowest notes you can reach, but the notes where the singer feels most comfortable, most at ease. Finding your true voice—your tessitura—is critical to becoming the best musical artist you can be.

My studies reminded me of when I was a boy and an avid singer. I participated in show choirs and sang at events all over town—and loved it. Then puberty hit. My voice changed. I never could seem to find the voice that fit me, my new tessitura. So I quit. Like so many others, I relegated myself to singing in the shower and quietly following along in worship service, but I don't really belt it out as I once did. I lost my voice.

When we think of the word *virtue* today, we often think of it in a negative sense, meaning "without sin" or "not giving in to impurity." However, in ancient Greek (and thus in the New Testament Scriptures) the word translated "virtue" meant something closer to "unique strength." The virtue of a thing was what it was good at or good for. So the virtue of a knife is its sharpness, the virtue of a spoon is its roundness, and so on. Each thing's virtue is different.

In that sense, your virtue is like your voice. It is your tessitura, your unique strength. Stated another way, your virtue is what makes you truly you. It is what reveals your true self as you were created to be by God and redeemed to be Christ.

Just as we have seen that the seven deadly sins are not just arbitrary rules God came up with but are vices that destroy our humanity and corrupt the image of God in us, so in the same way, the seven cardinal virtues are those traits that equip and enable our true humanity to shine brightly, as God intended. They make us who we really are.

In his excellent book *The Power of Habit*, Charles Duhigg argues that "you can't extinguish a bad habit, you can only change it."[1] We're all creatures of habit, our brains hardwired to lock in repetitive behavior patterns. As a result, telling ourselves to "just say no" to a bad habit rarely helps; we need to replace the bad habit with a good habit. The apostle Paul takes this approach in Colossians 3, urging us to "put on" positive traits such as truth and love every time he instructs us to "put off" a negative trait such as lying or rage. In other words, we need to replace vices with virtues.

We have already touched on the virtues in the course of going through the seven deadly sins, but in this chapter we'll unfold them a little more and focus in on the practical, everyday things we can do as parents to nurture and develop these virtues. We want to boost the virtue volume in our sons and daughters so they never lose their songs.

1. Humility.

Humility is the opposite of pride, but it may be the most misunderstood of the seven virtues. Humility is not the same thing as poor self-image or low self-esteem. As Rick Warren put it, "Humility is not thinking less of yourself; it is thinking of yourself less."[2] Humility is what happens when we open our eyes to how amazing, beautiful, and interesting other people can be.

I'm a baseball guy. For a ballplayer, there are a lot of stance adjustments you can make to improve your swing, including appropriately placing your feet, bending your knees, lifting your elbow, leveling your swing, rotating your hips. All of those things take work. However, the single most critical factor is the simple advice every coach gives a beginning player on day one: keep your eye on the ball. As important as all the factors are that are within yourself, by far the most important is to keep your focus on the thing that is outside yourself, and that is the ball.

Life is the same way. We all need to improve in many ways, and there's nothing wrong with working on ourselves. However, we were designed by God to love Him and love others. So our whole swing gets out of whack if all we think about is ourselves. To make it work, we need to keep our eyes on others.

The best way to do this is to become a cheerleader for other people. Teach your children to look for the good in others, take an interest in their strengths and abilities, and verbalize praise and encouragement for their achievements. Remember, humility does not come from trying to think poorly of yourself; it comes from thinking good of others. Of course, the best way to teach your children to encourage others is for you to encourage them. Model a healthy balance of praise to criticism—which is about ten parts positive for every one part negative.

Here's the interesting thing about self-image that happens to children who learn to be cheerleaders for others—their own self-esteem is lifted. This happens for two reasons. First, by looking for things to praise in others, kids begin to notice that everyone is different. Not everyone has the same set of strengths. This is a key discovery that allows them to discover and accept their own unique set of strengths.

Second, by constantly practicing encouragement even when others get down, children learn the vital skill of self-compassion. To illustrate, let's go back to baseball. First, imagine a player who constantly critiques other players and puts them down. What happens to that child when he gets up to the plate? The same condemning, criticizing voices he used on others starts to tear him apart inside his own head whenever he misses a pitch. Pretty soon he has a bleacher full of hecklers in his own mind everywhere he goes, telling him, "You're a loser, you can't do it, you're worthless."

In contrast, imagine a player who is constantly speaking words of encouragement to her teammates: "You can do it! Shake it off. You'll get the next one! Don't worry about that swing, just wait for your pitch!" What happens to that child when she gets to the plate? The same chorus of affirming voices can now be applied to herself, lifting her self-image and inspiring her to not give up.

This is the core teaching of Jesus about relationships—"judge not and you won't be judged"—only this time it is applied to your relationship with yourself. Self-compassion is the vital skill of learning to cut yourself some slack, to forgive yourself for weaknesses, imperfections, and shortcomings, and to celebrate your own unique set of gifts. The way we learn that skill, like any other, is through practice. In this case, when we practice humility with others by being a cheerleader, we reap the ability to accept ourselves.

To nurture humility, practice being your children's biggest cheerleader, and then teach them how to be a cheerleader for others.

2. Chastity.

Chastity is the opposite of lust. To be clear, the virtue of chastity is much more than not lusting, in the same way that being healthy means much more than not drinking poison. In the ancient traditions, the practice of chastity included fully developing yourself physically, mentally, and emotionally.

Think of lust as you would cancer: If it takes hold, radical steps are necessary to eradicate it. As Jesus said (speaking metaphorically), "If your right eye causes you to sin, tear it out."[3] However, chastity is like cultivating good health. It includes many positive behaviors such as developing friendships, bettering your mind through education, and embracing a worthwhile purpose in life.

Of course, it is important to teach our sons and daughters to make a commitment to God's plan for sexual purity. However, in addition to teaching them when to say no, I also want a strategy that includes giving them a lot of things to say yes to, which means helping them discover a bigger world to engage in.

As parents it's easy to miss how important boredom is when it comes to lust. Sure, physical temptations are real, especially for teens filled with their legendary raging hormones. However, as often as not, the thing that actually gets them in trouble is not so much desire as simply being curious and not having anything better to do than mess around.

Proverbs has something to say about this. The great king advises his son, "Say to wisdom, 'You are my sister,' and call insight your intimate friend, to keep you from the forbidden woman, from the adulteress with her smooth words."[4]

In other words, those who are engaged in the pursuit of wisdom are naturally kept away from the tempting power of lust.

I would suggest that one of the best ways of nurturing chastity in our sons and daughters is to create an interesting world for them through challenging educational experiences that expose them to new ideas. Take them to museums, art galleries, state parks, sporting events, and on spontaneous adventures. Travel with them. Try new things together. When they enthusiastically discover their interests, fan and fuel them into flames. Never speak of education as a drudgery they should look forward to being done with when they grow up; instead, teach them to be lifelong learners and students of life.

Sex and our other physical drives are wonderful, powerful parts of life, but they grow out of proportion when we allow the others aspects of life—mental, emotional, and spiritual—to grow weak through negligence. The wise parent keeps an eye out for all the warning signs of lust and takes due precautions to protect their sons and daughters from impurity, but they doesn't stop there. Wise parents also encourage the healthy, vibrant life of the mind and body that is what chastity is all about.

To nurture chastity, engage your son or daughter in a wider world through new and interesting ideas and experiences that encourage a healthy, vital life of body, mind, and spirit.

3. Kindness.

Kindness, the virtue that opposes envy, is not the same thing as its socially manufactured substitute, niceness. Especially here in the South, everyone is nice to you, even when they hate your guts. True kindness is to niceness what good old-fashioned cane sugar is to artificial sweeteners. A little of the real stuff goes a long way, and it doesn't leave a bitter aftertaste as the fakes do.

There's an actual city called Niceville near where I grew up in Florida. However, I think a lot of Christians live in an imaginary city of Niceville, and by looking at their behavior you'd have to conclude they were running for office there. When you meet a person who is working toward becoming the mayor of Niceville, you get the sense he is *thinking* about himself even as he *does* things for you. Although he may do you favors that are supposedly free gifts, you still walk away feeling as if you owe him something.

If we attempt to teach our children to act kindly without cultivating the true spirit of kindness, it will feel like a burden to them—a load of guilt rather than a free gift. On the other hand, true kindness is an incredible opportunity for joy. Where envy robs us of happiness (Proverbs says it "rots the bones"), giving kindness to others is simultaneously a gift of life to ourselves. When you're having a bad day, it's amazing how much pausing and doing something genuinely kind for someone else can lift your mood. Somehow, getting out of yourself is like hitting a reset button on your attitude.

To cultivate the virtue of kindness, I see three key parts: first, be a noticer; second, become empowered; and third, offer a personal touch. Being a noticer simply means we notice little things about other people that are signals to their struggles—symptoms of pain, anxiety, fear, and stress. Just as humility comes from recognizing the strengths and abilities of others, so kindness flows out of recognizing their hurts and sorrows. As my older daughter said to me one day, "People aren't projects; people are people." A noticer treats people as people.

Being empowered means we believe we can do something to help. So often we simply don't act on what we notice because we don't believe we can make a difference. A kind person doesn't think about what can't be done, but what can. We don't have to solve everyone else's problems to make life a little easier for them.

Offering a personal touch is often literally just that—a touch, whether a pat on the back, a quick hug, or a helping hand. Touch is an extremely powerful bonding and healing agent between human beings. Other times, touch is the action we take to personalize kindness—writing and mailing a sympathy note or remembering someone's favorite flavor of coffee creamer.

For several years, our church's youth group has made an effort when they go on their winter discipleship retreat to include a mission project, serving a group home for children nearby. One of the things our team noticed was, whereas teens from our church often had personalized items, none of the kids in the orphanage had anything with their name on it. Our team made it a goal to give each student a duffel bag embroidered with his or her name. For some, it was the first time they had ever owned a personalized item. Because our team members were noticers, felt empowered to act, and put a personal touch on their action, those bags went a long way toward building new relationships with teens who were in need.

To nurture kindness, guide your children to notice the little things that make life difficult or uncomfortable for others, and then empower them to act in simple but personal ways to brighten the days of others.

4. Charity.

Charity is love in action. I hesitate to use the word because it has so often been misused. In particular, we want to avoid what author Robert Lupton calls toxic charity—the giving away of handouts in a manner that creates dependency between the receiver and the giver and thus reduces the dignity of the person we are supposedly helping.[5] However, if we can recover the true meaning of the word, we will discover a rich and multilayered concept that can add much to our lives.

Remember, the corresponding vice—greed—is not about the money; it's about the me. Likewise, charity is not really about the gift; it's about the relationship between the giver and the receiver. Is it a one-time, impersonal transaction or an ongoing, personal investment?

True charity is a lot like choosing stock. When you buy stock, you are purchasing a stake in the success of a company. When they do well, you do well. When they lose money, so do you. You don't buy stock based merely on how well a company is doing today but based on how well you think they will do in the future—what their growth prospects are.

Thus, when Jesus says, "Store up for yourselves treasures in heaven,"[6] He is encouraging us to invest our time and energy in the places that will earn the most lasting rewards. The way to do that is to invest in people, because people are the only things that will last into eternity.

Charity is seeing the potential in people. It is planting a seed where you believe a fruit tree can grow. It is an act of faith—a belief that people can grow and change and develop into something amazing, and nothing is more rewarding than seeing that potential come to fruition.

So nurturing charity in our children begins with helping them visualize people's potential. Share with them biographies of people who accomplished great things, and focus attention on those who helped them early on. Help them to imagine how rewarding it must have been to be Thomas Edison's science teacher or Babe Ruth's coach. Of course, every person you invest in won't become world renowned, but the point is the same—we multiply our own joy by investing in the future joy of others.

I have a hobby of collecting paintings. One of my favorite things to do is to find a relatively unknown artist who is just starting out and who I think (with my limited knowledge of art) has potential to become a master. I don't want to just buy from those everyone can see are great artists; I want the satisfaction of knowing I bought their work—and thus supported their development—when they were just beginning to bloom.

In the same way, I want to teach my children to decorate their lives with "early paintings" of their own—acts of charity, gifts of love, attention, time, and yes, even money, invested in the lives of others in a way that says, "I believe in you and in who you can become." Seeing others bloom, and knowing you had an hand in helping them grow, is a source of great joy.

To nurture charity, help your sons and daughters identify the potential in others, and invest in that potential with their time, energy, and money.

5. Temperance.

Temperance is the Goldilocks virtue: "not too hot, not too cold, but just right!" Frankly, that seems a little boring. We know we should be more temperate, we know that too much of anything can be bad for us ... but hot and cold both seem so much more fun than lukewarm.

The law of diminishing returns says, past a certain point, the rewards of any given behavior always become less and less. The high the addict used to get from one dose now requires a double dose. Then triple. The returns diminish.

The hard part—for ourselves and for our children—is remembering that truth when we've just experienced pleasure. We know that, at some point, if we eat enough doughnuts, we'll get sick of them. But right after you eat that first doughnut, all you can think about is, if one is good, two are better!

Let me make a bold claim: there is no such thing as pure self-control. No one can consistently, by willpower alone, resist the immediate lure of *more* for the long-term value of *enough*. But that's only because we think of temperance the wrong way, as a solo virtue.

Temperance is a social virtue. It's not really about self-control; it's about us-control. It's not willpower; it's we-power! In other words, the only way to successfully nurture the virtue of temperance over the long haul is to surround ourselves with others who share the same goals. We all know the destructive influence the wrong friends can have when it comes to the vice of gluttony, but we overlook the life-giving influence the right friends can have.

I think there are two reasons we don't make better use of positive peer pressure to help us achieve a balanced life. First, we have spiritual pride. We think it somehow makes us a better Christian if we can say, "All I need is Jesus to live right." It's true that all you need is Jesus—but the way Jesus has chosen to make Himself available to us on earth is through His hands and feet, the body of Christ, the church. I'd hate to think where I might be today without the small group of men I've met with on Thursday mornings for years who have offered accountability to help keep me on track.

The second reason we don't make use of positive peer pressure is we don't learn the tools for authentic Christian community. How does it happen that one friend continues to destroy his health with overeating, drugs, alcohol, or another form of intemperance, even as the rest of the group pursues a healthy lifestyle? The devastating answer is a conspiracy of silence. We're too proud, ashamed, and afraid to ask for accountability from our friends, and they are too nice to confront us even when the symptoms of intemperance become perfectly visible.

So if we want to nurture temperance in our children, we need to teach them how to choose friends wisely and teach them the courage and conversation skills it takes to have true accountability between friends. Role-play with them how to ask friends to keep them accountable for making wise choices. Then role-play what to say when they need to confront a friend who might be getting out of line with potentially destructive habits. And of course, model all of this for them by doing the same things with your own friends in front of them. Imagine the lifelong impact it could have on a son or daughter if they heard one of your friends challenge you to put down that extra doughnut or beer, not out of a spirit of judgment but out of genuine love and concern. They would say to themselves, "That's what friends do." And they would be right.

To nurture the virtue of temperance in your children, teach them how to make friends and be the kind of friend who thrives on healthy accountability.

6. Diligence.

Diligence means working with your full energy in order to reach your full potential. You can't halfheartedly become a whole person.

When it comes to work, it's all about whom you are working for. Some people work hard, but only when the boss is watching. They can't seem to generate energy without some external source prodding them on, so they fall short of their potential unless constantly supervised.

Others work hard for themselves but then go too far and burn out or become workaholics. While it's true a job well done is its own reward, if we have only ourselves to please, we never quite know when the job is done well enough. We never have that sense of peace that comes from hearing someone say, "Well done, good and faithful servant ... Enter into the joy of your master."[7] Work quickly falls into the trap of perfectionism, the self-destructive treadmill of *never enough*.

Instead, our aim should be for our children to recognize that the true goal of all work is to glorify God. As Paul wrote to some of the early Christians, "Work willingly at whatever you do, as though you were working for the Lord rather than for people. Remember, the Lord will give you an inheritance as your reward, and the Master you are serving is Christ."[8]

When you teach your children to work for the Lord—whether it's elementary tasks like brushing their own teeth or cleaning their own room, or applying themselves in academics or athletics, or taking on their first part-time job—you provide them with an amazing source of joy. God always sees us, He is always pleased by the effort to do our best, and He will always reward us. To know that is to have a continual source of meaning and satisfaction regardless of the world around us.

Parents tend to underestimate the power they have to motivate work through praise. Children have an innate desire to please their parents[9] but that desire is also delicate; it can be easily crushed when the only feedback they get is negative, or worse, when they get no feedback at all. Too often, we simply assume our children know we are pleased with their work if we don't tell them otherwise. Notice how specific the writer of Proverbs is with his son: "My child, if your heart is wise, my own heart will rejoice! Everything in me will celebrate when you speak what is right."[10]

He doesn't leave any doubt in his son's mind: If you do this, it will make me happy. I'll be pleased. I'll be proud of you. A child who knows that will move heaven and earth to do it.

To be effective, praise needs to be expressed openly, frequently, and consistently. It also needs to be specific. Just saying "You did a great job" is not particularly helpful. When you give concrete examples, you make your praise actionable. Again, your children will naturally want to please you, but they can't do it if they don't know what they did right so they can do it again.

The ultimate point, of course, is not for your children to please you (or their teachers, coaches, or future bosses) but for them to transfer that desire to please from you to their heavenly Father, as we read in the New Testament: "For our earthly fathers disciplined us for a few years, doing the best they knew how. But God's discipline is always good for us, so that we might share in his holiness."[11]

We're bound to make mistakes in our parenting, but if we can give our children confidence they are capable of doing meaningful work that makes us proud and ultimately gives glory to God, we will put them a long way down the road toward developing the diligence they need to ensure they don't waste their God-given potential.

To nurture the virtue of diligence, give frequent, specific, positive feedback to your children every time they use their energy for work.

7. Patience.

Patience is the last virtue, and in many ways, it is the virtue that makes all the other virtues work. No matter how we look at it, becoming the person God created us to be always takes one thing: time. And time seems like the one thing we all hate to give.

Childhood seems like the hardest stage of life in which to be patient. Probably the most famous question asked by every child on a vacation road trip is, "Are we there yet?" We're so focused on the destination that the journey seems to be nothing but pure torture.

And yet God has designed so much of life to take place in the journey. I love the illustration of tree roots. Trees that are watered too frequently have shallow roots that can easily become sick, dry up in a drought, or blow over in high winds. Those that have to wait to be watered grow deeper, so they are healthier, stronger, and can endure storms.

In the same way, our children will either pass or fail the tests of life as adults based on the strengths they develop through patiently enduring times of suffering and waiting today. In that sense, we can draw a strange kind of joy out of being put into difficult circumstances. As James puts it, "Dear brothers and sisters, when troubles of any kind come your way, consider it an opportunity for great joy. For you know that when your faith is tested, your endurance has a chance to grow. So let it grow, for when your endurance is fully developed, you will be perfect and complete, needing nothing."[12]

So how do we help our children develop patience? In this case, I think it is not so much a matter of what we do as what we don't do. No parent likes to see his or her child suffer. However, if we're too quick to rush in and remove any discomfort, we can rob our children of the maturing power of trials. If we never allow them to struggle, to wait, or to endure, we doom them to a life of immaturity and diminish their potential for joy.

In the final analysis, this comes down to faith. When what we see in front of us is a child who is hurting, it's only natural that we do anything in our power to remove the cause. Only if we see, through eyes of faith, the future accomplishment and joy that will come to them through endurance, can we have the wisdom it takes to teach them patience.

As I write this, the 2014 Winter Olympics are underway, and Procter and Gamble has been running a tear-jerking series of television commercials about the mothers of Olympic athletes. The videos start with series of images showing moms who nurture their kids through falls, bumps, bruises, and even painful injuries. But then the videos take a turn, and we see those same children, older now, reaching the pinnacle of their sports, competing on the world stage in the Olympics, and we see the joy on their mothers' faces when their children ultimately triumph. The closing tag says, "For teaching us that falling only makes us stronger. Thank you, Mom."

That's what patience is all about: Believing that struggle—and pain—are not only necessary evils in a fallen world but are actually doorways through which we enter into our greatest joys. For the Christian, that belief is based on our trust that our God loves us enough not to allow anything to come our way that He cannot use for our greater good. The truth of the often-quoted verse, "God causes everything to work together for the good of those who love God and are called according to his purpose for them," finds its foundation in another verse from the same chapter. "I am convinced that nothing can ever separate us from God's love. Neither death nor life, neither angels nor demons, neither our fears for today nor our worries about tomorrow—not even the powers of hell can separate us from God's love."[13]

To nurture the virtue of patience, put before your children a vision of a God so loving and trustworthy that they will know He is always working for their good even in the midst of their greatest suffering and pain.

These seven virtues are seven paths to becoming the individuals God created us to be while helping our sons and daughters to do the same. Underlying all of them is the God of love who is faithful to complete the good works He began in us, from the moment He planned our births until eternity.

Chapter 10

WHAT IF IT'S TOO LATE?

"I wish you were dead. The only thing I want from you is your money. Give me what's coming to me now, and I'm out of here." The day your teenage son looks you in the eye and says something like that, you might feel like a failure as a parent. But in case you've forgotten or haven't read it lately, that's exactly what happens to the father in Jesus's famous parable of the Prodigal Son.[1]

It's a beautiful story of redemption and love, but it's also a reminder that even for the best parents, there's no guarantee your children will turn out the way you hope they will. The breathtaking thing about loving children is that, ultimately, it's up to them what they do with their lives. That's both terrifying and wonderful.

Of course, since the cutting edge of Jesus's parable is to show what's wrong with the other son—the firstborn, rule follower, good boy who does everything he's told but who also never understands grace, forgiveness, mercy, nor love—the parable is also a thought-provoking reminder that parenting is about more than making sure your children don't end up in jail or pregnant or on drugs. It's about shaping the heart.

If I've communicated anything in this book, I hope it's that both the vices that misshape our hearts and the virtues that nurture them flow out of the innermost part of our being. Parenting is not about policies and procedures. It's about becoming the kind of people we would like to reproduce.

So what do you do if you believe you've already ruined your child's life? As we've journeyed through the seven deadly sins, perhaps you've seen how one or more of them has dominated your own heart. And perhaps you've looked in the mirror of your son's or daughter's eyes and had that sinking feeling in the pit of your stomach that says, "They are going to turn out just like me—and that's not a good thing."

As parents, we often tell our children that we can see the future. We've gone down the road before them and we know where it's going to end. We tell them this to warn them and convince them to listen to our wisdom and learn from our mistakes. But that prophetic ability to see what's coming quickly turns into a curse when they refuse to listen to us. Is there anything more painful in the world than knowing your child is doing something that will hurt and there's nothing you can do to stop it?

If that's where you find yourself today, let me offer three slices of encouragement. First, every parent has regrets. All of us fail. No parent looks at his child and says, "Yep, I did that a hundred percent right" (at least, no parent who isn't blinded by incredible arrogance and an ego the size of an SUV).

Second, where you are headed matters more than where you have been. No matter how old your children are, the most important thing you can do for them is to set an example of the kind of person they should be. That starts by your willingness to repent, to turn around, to make changes, and to start something new in your life, no matter how much you may have messed up in the past.

That doesn't mean there aren't scars. Life is like a book written in permanent ink. You can't erase the previous chapter. However, you can change the ending by adding new chapters. Children need to know later chapters can be different.

My coauthor Ken had a grandfather, Charles, who was an alcoholic. He left his family, remarried, and had several more children, but he was not the best dad to them, either. Later in life, though, he sobered up and became active in Alcoholics Anonymous. As a sponsor, he helped scores of people turn their lives around. To them, he was a hero. He wrote a second chapter to his life.

Not all of Charles's children made peace with him before he died. To some, his work in AA did not make up for his failures as a father and husband. But imagine the alternatives. Charles could have stayed a drunk. He could have sobered up but spent the rest of his life regretting his past. Either way, he couldn't undo the damage that had already been done. But because he did what he did—because he turned his life around and did what he could to help others with what time he had left—his children have a model to know that no matter what they do or how far they may fall in life, they can always write a second chapter. If you can show your children that grace is always possible and hope is real, that is a powerful legacy.

God may be calling you to write a second chapter by changing how you raise your younger children after you realize you've made mistakes with your older ones. Being willing to make course corrections not only benefits the younger ones, it demonstrates to the older ones you are not too proud to learn. Maybe your second-chapter calling is to do things differently with your grandchildren. If you weren't there the way you feel you should have been for your kids, you can't make up for it with grandchildren, but you can still do a lot of good—again, not only in the lives of your grandchildren but also, indirectly, in the lives of your children, whether they acknowledge it or not. If you are divorced and remarried, your second chapter may be to work hard on making your second marriage succeed. Children often resent a stepparent, fairly or unfairly, for taking the place of their birth parent, but in the long run they benefit from seeing that marriage can work.

Perhaps your second chapter is to invest in the lives of other people's children. My boss's wife, Virginia Thompson, has a great relationship with their three adult daughters. However, she realized when they moved away to other cities that she couldn't invest as much time with them as she might have wanted. Instead of feeling disappointed, she started a small group for young women her daughters' ages in our church, and it has developed into an incredible ministry. The way she explains it, "I'm trusting that if I invest in the young women that are around me, the Lord will see to it that someone else invests in my daughters' lives in their cities in ways that I can't because of the distance between us." For Virginia, that distance is physical, not emotional, but the same principle could hold true for you if years of painful memories have estranged you from your kids. Invest in whom you can invest in. Trust God for the results.

Which brings me to my third word of encouragement: Our heavenly Father loves your children even more than you do. You can trust him with their future. Remember, parenthood is a temporary trust. We are given oversight of our children for a time, not so we can always care for them but so we can lead them to a relationship with the One who will always care for them. And though we will certainly let them down—even ruin their lives, at least in our own minds—God will never let our children down, in the long run. He knew all about our shortcomings and weaknesses when He entrusted them to us, and He can use even our failures for good.

My parents and stepparents made their share of mistakes with me. I made more than my share with them. Yet God still got hold of me. Or I should say, He continues to get hold of me—forming me, shaping me, fathering me into the son he wants me to be. I have to remind myself of this when I begin to worry about my children and their future. The time will come when they will be out of my reach, but they will never be out of His.

Along with those three words of encouragement, let me offer four pieces of advice for those who feel they have ruined their child's life.

1. Apologize and ask forgiveness if it is appropriate.
Remember, the first and greatest vice is pride; the first and greatest virtue is humility. When you are willing to apologize for past wrongs, it is not a sign of weakness; it is the key to unlocking God's power and grace.

2. Take an inventory of your promises.
Your word is a powerful force with your children, but that power is destroyed when your word is broken. Often our children feel we have betrayed a promise without us even realizing it. We speak idle words, and they take it as an ironclad guarantee. Your children have an amazing ability to forget your instructions but remember your promises! That time you told your ten-year-old son you'd take him

fishing, but you got busy at work and forgot? He remembers that as if it were yesterday, even though he can't seem to remember to pick up his dirty socks lying on the floor. And that memory can become a root of bitterness, undermining his relationship with you (and perhaps undermining his confidence in God as well).

The solution is simply to ask them: "Has there ever been a time I made you a promise and didn't keep it?" Then be quiet and listen. Listen from the heart, without defensiveness. It may be there is nothing you can do now except sincerely apologize. But if you can, show each child you'll do everything in your power to keep your promise, even now. It wouldn't be the worst thing in the world to take your thirty-year-old son on a fishing trip.

3. Find friends for the journey.

Parenting was never meant to be done alone. You and your spouse need the reinforcement of other parents facing the same struggles and striving after the same goals as you. Get involved in a church, and join a small group where you can nurture authentic relationships and do life together. Connect with families at the same stage of life you are in, so you will know you aren't the only ones struggling with a defiant toddler, a forgetful child, or a moody teenager. But also connect with families who are a stage or two ahead of you. Find someone who can mentor you, warn you of pitfalls, and encourage you. No one's perfect, and no one has all the answers, but we're all stronger when we rely on one another. That's what the church is—one big family of faith, made up of many earthly families mutually supporting one another and pointing one another to Christ.

4. Finally, have fun.

Sing, dance, laugh, play. Don't be afraid to embrace the joy. Parenthood is the great adventure! When I remember that fateful day I scratched the side of my wife's van on the concrete column of the beach condominium, after all was said and done, after all my pride and all my mistakes, it's easy to forget we got to our destination safely. We got to play and swim and go for walks together, and I got to see the big, beautiful world through the eyes of my son, daughters, and foster son. That was truly a gift from God.

That's when I realize: I haven't ruined my children's lives. God is using their lives to make my life complete.

NOTES

Chapter 1: I've Got This

1. Not his real name. For legal and security reasons, the identities of children in the foster care system are kept private.
2. Proverbs 3:5 NRSV.
3. Proverbs 26:12 NRSV.
4. Luke 6:37–38 NRSV.
5. Luke 6:39–40 NRSV.

Chapter 2: I'm Not the Problem

1. Proverbs 3:34; James 4:6; 1 Peter 5:5.
2. Henri J. M. Nouwen, *In the Name of Jesus* (New York: Crossroad, 2002), 77.
3. Jeremiah 17:9.
4. Luke 6:41–42 NRSV.
5. 1 John 1:8. On this topic I highly recommend the little book *Leadership and Self-Deception*, Arbinger Institute (San Francisco: Berrett-Koehler, 2010).
6. Proverbs 9:8.
7. See John 13.

Chapter 3: If It Feels Good, It Must Be Good

1. Not their real names.
2. Matthew 7:11.
3. Genesis 1:31.
4. See John 21.
5. Hebrews 11:6.
6. John Piper, *Desiring God* (Colorado Springs, CO: Multnomah, 2003).
7. Romans 1:21–25.
8. 1 Thessalonians 4:3–8.
9. Sources at www.xxxchurch.com/stats have resources and tools for anyone seeking help with a pornography addiction.
10. David's story is found in the Bible in the book of 2 Samuel.
11. Galatians 6:1 NLT.
12. For an overview see "The addicted brain," *Harvard Health Publications*, June 9, 2009, www.health.harvard.edu/newsweek /The_addicted_brain.html.
13. Romans 8:31–32 NLT.
14. Proverbs 24:16.
15. 2 Timothy 2:22 NKJV.
16. Stephen Arterburn and Fred Stoeker, *Every Man's Battle: Winning the War on Sexual Temptation One Victory at a Time* (Colorado Springs, CO: WaterBrook, 2000).
17. Shannon Ethridge, *Every Woman's Battle: Discovering God's Plan for Sexual and Emotional Fulfillment* (Colorado Springs, CO: WaterBrook, 2008).
18. John 10:10.

Chapter 4: Focus on What You Don't Have

1. Matthew 6:25.
2. Matthew 6:27.
3. Matthew 6:28–30.
4. 2 Corinthians 10:12 NLT.
5. Ephesians 4:12–13.
6. Colossians 3:10.
7. "Every good gift and every perfect gift is from above, coming down from the Father of lights" (James 1:17).
8. Andy Stanley and Lane Jones, *Communicating for Change: Seven Keys to Irresistible Communication* (Colorado Springs, CO: WaterBrook Multnomah, 2006), 111.
9. Genesis 1:31.
10. 1 John 4:8.
11. Romans 8:28 NASB.
12. Romans 12:15.
13. Proverbs 14:30.
14. Marcus Buckingham and Donald O. Clifton, *Now, Discover Your Strengths* (New York: Gallup Organization audio book, 2001).

Chapter 5: It's All about Me

1. Mark 8:34–37.
2. Matthew 6:24.
3. Henri J. M. Nouwen, *The Return of the Prodigal Son: A Story of Homecoming* (New York: Doubleday, 1994), 131.
4. Psalm 115:4–8.
5. Luke 6:30–31.

6. 1 John 4:20.

7. Romans 8:29.

8. Ephesians 4:28.

9. Jessica Jackley, "Poverty, money—and love," TED Talks, July 2010, 18:33, www.ted.com/talks/jessica_jackley_poverty_money_and_love.

Chapter 6: You Always Need More!

1. "Overweight and Obesity," Centers for Disease Control and Prevention, accessed February 2, 2015, www.cdc.gov/obesity/data/facts.html.

2. Bill Hybels, Willow Creek Global Leadership Summit talk, 2013.

3. Luke 6:20–21.

4. Colossians 3:2.

5. Matthew 6:10.

6. Psalm 89:11; 108:5.

7. 2 Corinthians 12:7–10.

8. Philippians 2:5–11.

9. Hebrews 12:2–3.

10. Ecclesiastes 3:1–2.

11. Andy Stanley, Catalyst Conference talk, 2012.

12. Matthew 6:16–18.

13. 1 Timothy 4:4.

14. 1 Thessalonians 5:16–18.

Chapter 7: The Easy Life Is the Good Life

1. Proverbs 6:6–11.

2. Psalm 127:2.

3. Matthew 11:30.

4. Charles E. Hummel, *Tyranny of the Urgent* (Downers Grove, IL: InterVarsity, 1997).

5. Stephen R. Covey, *The Seven Habits of Highly Effective People* (New York: Simon & Schuster, 1990), 159.

6. Proverbs 13:4; 21:25; 15:19; 22:13.

7. Proverbs 26:16.

8. 2 Kings 13:19.

9. Luke 12:48.

10. Psalm 42:3–6.

11. Psalm 42:9–11.

12. 1 Corinthians 15:58.

13. Colossians 3:21 NASB.

14. Psalm 73:26.

15. Joshua 1:9.

Chapter 8: If You Don't Get Your Way, Get Mad!

1. Genesis 1:26.

2. Psalm 8:3–6 NASB.

3. Proverbs 21:3 NASB.

4. Micah 6:8.

5. Isaiah 1:11, 13–17 NASB.

6. Romans 2:1.

7. Luke 6:39.

8. To be clear, the Torah says a great deal about God's forgiveness, but it does not put forgiveness of others front and center the way the teaching of Jesus does.

9. Galatians 3:24 NASB.

10. Matthew 5:21–22.

11. James 3:5–10.

12. Ephesians 4:26–27.

13. Matthew 6:12, 14–15.

14. Ephesians 4:32; see also Colossians 3:13; Matthew 18:35.

Chapter 9: Becoming Who You Are

1. Charles Duhigg, *The Power of Habit: Why We Do What We Do in Life and Business* (New York: Random House, 2012), 62.

2. Rick Warren, *The Purpose Driven Life* (Grand Rapids, MI: Zondervan, 2002), 148.

3. Matthew 5:29.

4. Proverbs 7:4–5.

5. Robert D. Lupton, *Toxic Charity: How Churches and Charities Hurt Those They Help (And How to Reverse It)* (New York: HarperOne, 2011).

6. Matthew 6:20 NASB.

7. Matthew 25:23.

8. Colossians 3:23–24 NLT.

9. See Proverbs 17:6.

10. Proverbs 23:15–16 NLT.

11. Hebrews 12:10 NLT.

12. James 1:2–4 NLT.

13. Romans 8:28, 38 NLT.

Chapter 10: What If It's Too Late?

1. See Luke 15:11–32.

QUESTIONS
FOR INDIVIDUAL
REFLECTION OR
GROUP DISCUSSION

CHAPTERS 1 AND 2: PRIDE

1. How would you define pride?

2. What does God's attitude toward pride reveal to you about His character? How do you see humility demonstrated by Jesus? See James 4:6.

3. Do you have any scratches or scars from times in your life when you told God or others, "I've got this; I don't need your help"? What have you learned from those experiences? See Proverbs 3:5 NRSV.

4. Which would you say that you tend to rely on more to influence your children: your authority and power or your influence through relationship?

5. Does it cause you concern that your children may become much like you when they are grown, or does it give you hope? What changes do you need to make in yourself to provide the best model for them?

6. Review the "Four Ways to Humble Yourself." What are some immediate actions you plan to take to help your children avoid pride? Are there long-term changes you need to begin making as well? Who will help hold you accountable to implement your plan?

CHAPTER 3: LUST

1. How would you define lust?

2. What does God's attitude toward lust reveal to you about His character? How do you see purity demonstrated by Jesus? See 1 Thessalonians 4:3–8.

3. Why is it important to communicate to our children that God is not opposed to pleasure? What messages about morality and pleasure are you sending to your children?

4. What have you learned from your own past struggles with lust and addictive behaviors? How are you finding the accountability and support that you need now?

5. How do you help your children avoid the trap of secret sins while allowing them appropriate

levels of privacy for their age? What additional safeguards do you think are necessary in today's digital world?

6. Review the "Three Steps to Breaking the Chain." Make a plan for how you will put one or more of these steps into action in your family, and share it with someone whom you can trust to support you.

CHAPTER 4: ENVY

1. How would you define envy?

2. What does God's attitude toward envy reveal to you about His character? How do you see acceptance demonstrated by Jesus?

3. Recall a time that you struggled with envy because you compared yourself with others. What can you learn from your experience that you could pass on to your children?

4. Do you know which aspects of their identities your children struggle to accept about themselves? How could you have a conversation with your children to uncover any self-rejection they are experiencing?

5. What language do you need to use more of to help your children learn to accept themselves and celebrate their strengths? What language do you need to use less often? See Colossians 3:10.

6. Review the "Eight Unenvious Steps." Pick one or two to try out in the next week, and then revisit the list to see if there are others you should implement.

CHAPTER 5: GREED

1. How do you define greed?

2. What does God's opposition to greed reveal to you about His character? How do you see generosity demonstrated by Jesus?

3. How has greed affected your relationships in the past? Share an example with your children of how you had to choose between focusing on people and focusing on things, and what you learned from that experience.

4. The deadly sin of greed has its roots in the fear of not having enough. What triggers that fear in your own heart? When do your

children most struggle with that fear? See
Matthew 6:25–27.

5. Review the "Three Greed Busters." Is there
one that stands out for your family to use?
Write down your strategy for putting it into
practice.

CHAPTER 6: GLUTTONY

1. How do you define gluttony?

2. What does God's opposition to gluttony
reveal to you about His character? How do you
see self-discipline demonstrated by Jesus?

3. How is it possible to be "blessed by less"?
Share an experience with your children when
you learned that you could actually experience
more joy by having less of something for a
season. See 2 Corinthians 12:7–10.

4. Does the concept of "rhythm" rather than
"balance" resonate with you as a way to bring
health to your family life? When is the last time
you evaluated your schedule to see if your life
is "in rhythm"?

5. Review the "Three Wolf Tamers." Set a date that you want to start using one of them, and ask your spouse or a friend to check in on your progress.

CHAPTER 7: SLOTH

1. How do you define sloth? See Proverbs 6:6–11.

2. What does God's opposition to sloth reveal to you about His character? How do you see diligence demonstrated by Jesus?

3. Have you had an experience when you either experienced a reward because of diligence or lost an opportunity due to laziness? Share what you learned with your children.

4. Would you say your children are like the ant— self-motivated by a greater purpose in life—or are they only motivated by external pressure? How can you help each of them gain a vision for a higher calling in life?

5. Have you or your children experienced a failure or loss that has caused you to give in to despair? How can you reawaken hope in your family? See Psalm 51:12.

6. Review the "Three Cups of Coffee." Brainstorm some creative ways to have a conversation with each of your children about at least one of these, and then pick one idea to put into action.

CHAPTER 8: WRATH

1. How would you define wrath? From God's point of view, what are the appropriate situations for "righteous anger"?

2. Have you ever thought of humanity (including yourself) as having a God-given responsibility to bring justice to the world? What experiences have you had with justice or injustice that could provide a teaching moment for your children? See Micah 6:8.

3. Do you need to apologize to anyone in your house for hurtful things you have said or done in an outburst of anger?

4. Are the rules in your house set up in a way that promotes the idea of justice to your children? Are there steps you need to take to make sure the rules are clear, the consequences are just, and the enforcement is consistent?

5. Review the "Three Temper Tamers." Ask yourself which one you most needed to hear for yourself and then which one might most apply to each of your children. Pray through your ideas and make a commitment to God to work on the one(s) that need work.

CHAPTER 9: THE VIRTUES

1. How would you define virtue? How would it reshape your parenting to think of virtue not merely as doing the right thing in the present but also as forming habits that shape whom your children will become tomorrow?

2. What does God's desire for His children to grow in virtue reflect about His character? How do you see the virtues perfected in Jesus? See Proverbs 23:15–16 NLT.

3. Trying to implement all seven virtues at one time could be overwhelming. How can you develop a plan for working through them gradually? Consider establishing a virtue of the week or month in your home. Brainstorm small ways you could reinforce that virtue through words and actions throughout that week or month.

4. Create a chart with all seven virtues, and post it on your refrigerator or some other visible place to track your progress. Consider keeping a virtues journal to record your journey and the life lessons you gain along the way.

CHAPTER 11: WHAT IF IT'S TOO LATE?

1. Do you have regrets about your parenting that are keeping you stuck in the past? Confessing our sins to God is always the first step, but verbalizing our mistakes to another person can sometimes help in gaining closure. Find a trusted friend or wise counselor with whom you can talk through your regrets, not so you can make excuses but so you can find the best ways to move forward.

2. How can you work through taking appropriate responsibility for your own failures and move forward into trusting God to "work all things together for good" (Romans 8:28) in your children's lives?

3. What "second chapter" calling is God putting in your heart? How are you responding to His loving offer of hope for the future?